M

MW01289986

KUTHUMI

Dictations received by the Messenger
Tatyana Nicholaevna Mickushina
from 2005 through 2013

UDC 141.339=111=03.161.1
BBC 87.7+86.4
M59

M59 Mickushina, T.N.

KUTHUMI.

Masters of Wisdom. – T.N. Mickushina. –
– 2018. – 216 pages. – (Series "Masters of Wisdom").

This book is a part of the Masters of Wisdom series.

This series of books presents a collection of Messages from different Masters who are most well-known to modern humanity. These Messages were transmitted through the Messenger Tatyana N. Mickushina, who has been working under the guidance of the Masters of Wisdom since 2004. Using a special method, T. N. Mickushina has received Messages from over 50 Beings of Light

This book contains Messages of Master Kuthumi. The Messages address new aspects of the Law of Karma, and provide a new understanding of the structure and evolution of man and the Universe, and raise the subtle psychological moments, the knowledge of which helps us to go through life.

ISBN-13: 978-1985645912
ISBN-10: 1985645912

Contents

Kuthumi *6*

You must aspire to control your thoughts and feelings
March 24, 2005 .... *25*

A Teaching on twin flames
April 26, 2005 .... *32*

We come to awaken your Divinity
May 8, 2005 .... *38*

Try to keep the state of inner peace and harmony during most of the day
Beloved Kuthumi May 19, 2005 .... *44*

A Teaching on karma
May 31, 2005 .... *51*

A Teaching on good Karma
June 6, 2005 .... *60*

There is a section of the Path that you will not be able to overcome alone without a guide
June 7, 2005 .... *67*

A Teaching on Buddha and the multiplying of the Buddha consciousness
June 14, 2005 .... *74*

A Teaching on the karma of inactivity

June 24, 2005 .... *82*

Are you ready to enter the Path?

June 29, 2005 .... *89*

A Teaching on karma descending at the end of the year

December 19, 2005 .... *96*

**Only when you receive the Law from within
your heart, do you become the executor of the Law**

April 28, 2006 .... *103*

Expanding the understanding of the Law of Karma

July 6, 2006 .... *109*

**You must constantly analyze the consequences
of your actions and try not to teach where your
teaching will be immediately dragged
through the mire**

December 26, 2006 .... *117*

A Teaching about your soul

January 6, 2007 .... *123*

Guidance for every day

June 26, 2007 .... *129*

**A Teaching about the necessity to keep your lower
bodies pure**

July 4, 2007 .... *135*

A Teaching on the liberation from karma

January 7, 2008 .... *141*

A Teaching on changing of vibrations

January 2, 2009 .... *147*

A Talk of vital importance

July 2, 2009 .... *152*

A Teaching on the liberation from negative energies

December 12, 2009 .... *157*

A Talk about the effect of the Messages

January 14, 2010 .... *164*

A Teaching on vibrations and the interconnection of everything that exists on Earth

June 12, 2010 .... *169*

Today's talk will explain to you the failures on your Path

December 28, 2010 .... *175*

You create your future and the future of the whole planet at the moment of conception of your child

June 17, 2011 .... *181*

Some comments on the Laws of Karma and Reincarnation

June 28, 2012 .... *187*

Divine Truth is comprehended not by external research but by inner searching

June 28, 2013 .... *192*

If you do not think about God, then you separate yourselves from God

December 26, 2013 .... *199*

The Path of a Mystic *206*

About the Messages and the Messenger *208*

Kuthumi[1]

Master Kuthumi had the name of Koot Hoomi Lal Singh in his last known incarnation. He is also known as K.H. He was a Kashmiri Brahman (Brahmin)[2] and lived for a long time in Samzhubzê, Tibet, in the 19th century. He was born in Punjab; his family had lived in Kashmir for many years. He traveled extensively, attending Oxford University in 1850 and studying at Leipzig University in Germany in the 1870s. During his stay in Leipzig, Kuthumi met Gustav Theodor Fechner, a philosopher and pioneer of modern psychological research methods.

---

[1] The text is based (except the paragraphs, where there are the references to other sources) on data from the book "The Human Aura," written by the Messengers Mark and Elizabeth Prophet under the dictation of the Master Kuthumi and Master Djwal Khul. See Kuthumi, Djwal Khul. The Human aura. – M.: Longfellow, 2003. – p. 285

[2] Brahmanas (obsolete. – Brahminas) is a group of the highest castes in India.

In 1875, at the suggestion of Kuthumi and El Morya, Helena Petrovna Blavatsky together with like-minded people founded the Theosophical Society. The Society preached the ideas of universal brotherhood and tolerance for all religions, in each of which the One Divine Self is manifested.

Koot Hoomi Lal Singh

The Teachings, which El Morya, Kuthumi, and other Adepts gave through Blavatsky, opened up ancient truths, which were foundational for both Eastern and Western religions. The Teachers tried to introduce humanity to the invisibly-working spiritual Brotherhood, aiming to facilitate the spiritual growth of humanity.

In his book *The Masters and the Path*, Charles Leadbeater, a well-known theosophist and a member of the Theosophical Society, mentions some details of the secluded life of his Master in Tibet:

"...Sometimes, too, He rests in His great armchair, and when His people see Him thus, they know that He must not be disturbed; they do not know exactly what He is doing, but suppose Him

H. Blavatsky, surrounded by the adepts (from left to right: Kuthumi, El Morya, Saint Germain)

to be in samadhi. The fact that people in the East understand this kind of meditation and respect it may be one of the reasons why the Adepts prefer to live there rather than in the West.

"In this way we get the effect of the Master sitting quietly for a considerable part of the day and, as we should say, meditating; but while He is apparently resting so calmly, He is in reality engaged all the time in the most strenuous labor on higher planes, manipulating various natural forces and simultaneously pouring forth influences of the most diverse character on thousands of souls. For the Adepts are the busiest people in the world. The Master, however, does much physical-plane work as well; He has composed some music and has written notes and papers for various purposes. He is also much interested in the growth of physical science, although this is especially the province of one of the other great Masters of the Wisdom.

"From time to time the Master Kuthumi rides on a big bay horse, and occasionally, when Their work lies together, He is accompanied by the Master

8

Morya, who always rides a magnificent white horse. Our Master regularly visits some of the monasteries and sometimes goes up a great pass to a lonely monastery in the hills. Riding in the course of His duties seems to be His principal exercise, but He sometimes walks with the Master Djwal Kul, who lives in a little cabin which He built with His own hands, quite near to the great crag on the way up to the plateau.

"Sometimes our Master plays on the organ which is in the large room in His house. He had it made in Tibet under His direction, and it is in fact a combined piano and organ, with a keyboard like those which we have in the West, on which He can play all of our Western music. It is unlike any other instrument with which I am acquainted, for it is in a sense double-fronted, as it can be played either from the sitting-room or the library. The principal keyboard (or rather the three keyboards: great organ, swell, and choir) is in the sitting-room, whereas the piano keyboard is in the library; and these keyboards can be used either together or separately.

"The full organ with its pedals can be played in the ordinary way from the sitting-room; but by turning a handle somewhat equivalent to a stop, the piano mechanism can be linked with the organ, so that it all plays simultaneously. From that point of view, in fact, the piano is treated as an additional stop on the organ.

"From the keyboard in the library, however, the piano can be played alone as a separate instrument, quite dissociated from the organ; but by some complicated mechanism the choir-organ is also linked to that keyboard, so that by it one can play the piano alone precisely as though it were an ordinary piano, or one can play the piano accompanied by the choir-organ, or at any rate by certain stops of that organ. It is also possible, as I said, to separate the two completely, and so, with a performer at each keyboard, to play a piano-organ duet. The mechanism and the pipes of this strange instrument occupy almost the whole of what might be called the upper story of this part of the Master's house. By magnetization He has placed it in communication with the Gandharvas, or Devas of music, so that whenever it is played they co-operate, and thus He obtains combinations of sound never to be heard on the physical plane; and there is, too, an effect produced by the organ itself as of an accompaniment of string and wind instruments.

"The song of the Devas is ever being sung in the world; it is ever sounding in men's ears, but they will not listen to its beauty.

"There is the deep drone of the sea, the sighing of the wind in the trees, the roar of the mountain torrent, the music of stream, river and waterfall, which together with many others form the mighty song of Nature as she lives. This is but the echo in the physical world of a far grander sound, that of the Being of the Devas. As is said in *Light on the Path*:

"Only fragments of the great song come to your ears while yet you are but man. But, if you listen to it, remember it faithfully, so that none which has reached you is lost, and endeavor to learn from it the meaning of the mystery which surrounds you. In time you will need no teacher. For as the individual has voice, so has that in which the individual exists. Life itself has speech, and is never silent. And its utterance is not, as you that are deaf may suppose, a cry; it is a song. Learn from it that you are part of the harmony; learn from it to obey the laws of the harmony."

"Every morning a number of people — not exactly pupils, but followers — come to the Master's house and sit on the veranda and outside it. Sometimes He gives them a little talk — a sort of lecturette; but more often He goes on with His work and takes no notice of them beyond a friendly smile, with which they seem equally contented. They evidently come to sit in His aura and venerate Him. Sometimes He takes His food in their presence, sitting on the veranda, with this crowd of Tibetans and others on the ground around Him; but generally He eats by Himself at a table in His room. It is possible that He keeps the rule of the Buddhist monks, taking no food after noon; for

I do not remember ever to have seen Him eat in the evening. It is even possible that He does not need food every day."

The correspondence of El Morya and Kuthumi to their disciples involved in the Theosophical Society, are published in *The Letters of Mahatmas* and other books. Some of these letters are kept in the collection of manuscripts in the British Museum.

Kuthumi keeps his focus on Samzhubzê/ Shigatse (the Masters and their Retreats), Tibet, where, playing his grand organ, the sacred flames of his heart evoke a cosmic harmony. Through his music, he bestows healing and peace around the entire planetary body and reaches the souls that go through a transition (including the death hour) and leads them to the ether retreats of the Great White Brotherhood to receive instructions in preparation for the following earthly lives. He inspires architects, poets, and scientists, awakening mystic memories about their own souls' harmony in the geometry and rhythm of stars.

Below, we enumerate some incarnations of Kuthumi:

In approximately 582-507 BC[3], he was **Pythagoras**, a Greek philosopher and mathematician, the "fair-haired Samian," who was regarded as the son of Apollo. Among others, he had a special gift: He remembered his previous incarnations. Here is what ancient philosophers Porphyry[4] wrote about it:

"... (according to Heraclides Ponticus,) Pythagoras used to say that in former times he was Aethalides and was regarded as a son of Hermes. Hermes offered him to choose any gift except immortality and Pythagoras asked to leave him, both alive and dead, a memory of what has happened to him. That is why during his life and in the moment of death he had the same memory. Subsequently, he became Euphorbus and was wounded by Menelaus. Euphorbus used to say that he had been Aethalides, that he had received a gift

---

[3] Other sources contain other dates of life of Pythagoras: from 586 to 580 - from 507 to 486 BC.

[4] Porphyry (232 or 234 - between 301 and 305) is a Neoplatonist philosopher, one of the most active members of the Plotinus circle; a student and a publisher of the works of Plotinus, the founder of Neoplatonism.

from Hermes, how his soul traveled, which animals and plants it had entered, what it had experienced in Aida, and what other souls experienced there." After Euphorbus's death, his soul entered Hermotimus, who came to Branchïdae to prove his memory of past lives and in the Temple of Apollo pointed at a shield that Menelaus dedicated to god. Euphorbus said: "Leaving the shore of Troy, Menelaus dedicated this shield to Apollo, but now it is all rotten, only ivory decoration is left." After Hermotimus's death, he became Pyrrhus, a Delian fisherman, and still remembered how he was Aethalides first, then Euphorbus, then Hermotimus. After Pyrrhus's death, he became Pythagoras and still kept the memory of everything mentioned above."[5]

In his book *Pythagoras's Life*, Porphyry narrates about other special qualities of Pythagoras

"...The same day, he was present in Italic Metapontum and Sicilian Tauromena, talking to his disciples in both places simultaneously. Everybody could prove that it is a long way between those cities by both land and sea, and it is impossible to cover this distance even over many days. It is generally known that Pythagoras showed Abaris the Hyperborean, a priest of Apollo, his golden hip

---

[5] Diogenes Laertius. About Life, Teachings, and Aphorisms of famous philosophers

to prove his words that Pythagoras was Apollo, the Hyperborean, himself. Once Pythagoras's friends were looking at a ship sailing by, guessing and estimating its cargo, and Pythagoras said: "You have a dead man!" He was right; a dead man happened to be on the ship. There exist countless other stories, even more divine and wondrous, which all show that no other man is spoken of as much and as extraordinarily as Pythagoras.

It is also known through word of mouth that he accurately predicted earthquakes, quickly stopped epidemics, averted rain-and hail-storms, and tamed rivers and sea waves to ensure a safe and easy passage for his fellow-travelers and himself. Empedokles, Epimenides, and Abaris adopted this ability of Pythagoras. As their poems prove, all of them performed the same miracles, which is why Empedokles was called the Windblocker: Epimenides the Purifier and Abaris the Windrunner, as if he had gotten an arrow from Apollo as a gift, on which he flew over impassible rivers and seas as if he had run in the air. Some people think that Pythagoras did the same, when one and the same day he spoke with his disciples in Metapontum and Tauromena. He soothed soul and body illnesses with singing and lyre playing; he taught his friends to do so too. He was able to hear even the harmony of the Universe, catching accords of all spheres and heavenly bodies moving within those spheres. We are not able to hear those accords because of the weakness of human nature."[6]

While a youth, Pythagoras associated with scholars and priests, passionately seeking scientific proof of the internal law, which was revealed to him in his meditation on Demeter — the Mother of The Earth. The search of the great synthesis of the truth first lead him to famous Greek philosophers of the time (Pherecydes, Herdomas, Anaximander, Thales) and then to the temples of Egypt, where he gained the trust of Memphis priests and was allowed into the mysteries of Isis in Thebes.

When Cambyses, an Asian military leader, violently invaded Egypt in about 529 BC, Pythagoras was exiled to Babylon. There, rabbis (Jewish Priests) revealed to him the secret teachings that had been given by Moses. Zoroastrian magi taught him music, astronomy, and the sacred science of appeals.

After twelve years in Babylon, Pythagoras left for Crotona, a populous Dorian port city located in the south of Italy now, and founded the brotherhood of the initiated. His "CITY OF THE CHOSEN"

---

[6] Yakov Krotov`s library [Electronic resource] / Diogenes Laertius. *About Life, Teachings, and Aphorisms of famous philosophers*. Available at: http://krotov.info/lib_sec/05_d/dio/gen_09.htm

was a school of the mysteries of the Great White Brotherhood. In Crotona, thoroughly chosen men and women followed a philosophy based on the mathematical expression of the Universal law, manifested in music, rhythm, and harmony of a life path characterized by strict discipline. After five years of testing by silence, Pythagoras's "mathematicians" went through a series of initiations, developing intuitive abilities of the heart. Due to these abilities, every God's son or daughter, as Pythagoras says in his Golden Poems, could become "the immortal wondrous God."

Pythagoras gave his teachings hidden from the sight of his disciples. He used a language of symbols that was understandable for only the most advanced disciples. The most significant theme for him was the fundamental understanding that number was the form and essence of creation. He formulated the basic parts of Euclidian geometry and developed astronomic views that eventually lead to Copernicus' Theory. According to chronicles, two thousand of Crotona's inhabitants gave up their habitual way of life and gathered together in Pythagoras's society under the wise rule of the Council of the Three Hundred(s) — an executive, scientific, and religious order that eventually had great political influence in Magna Graecia.

His doctrines influenced a great number of philosophers.

Pythagoras, "a restless adept," was ninety years old when Cylon, who was refused admission to the school of mysteries, instigated persecution of the philosopher. Facing the charges of Croton, Cylon read out loud Pythagoras's secret book, *Hieros Logo* (The Sacred Word), distorting and ridiculing the teachings. When Pythagoras and forty head-members of the order held council, Cylon set the building where the council took place on fire. Everyone in the building, except two people, died. As a result, the society disintegrated and most of the teaching was lost. However, the Teacher influenced many great philosophers including Plato, Aristotle, Augustine, Thomas Aquinas, and Francis Bacon.

Kuthumi was **Balthazar**, first century AD, one of the three Magi (astronomers and adepts), who followed the star (I AM Presence) of the Baby-Son, delivered by Virgin Mary, and who made a trip from the East to do honors to Baby-Jesus. There is a hypothesis that he was king of Ethiopia and brought Christ the treasures of his country — the gift of incense.

Kuthumi was also **Saint Francis of Assisi** (about 1181-1226, Italy). He was a founder of the Order of Saint Francis and a divine mendicant, who rejected family and treasures and was betrothed with "Madame Poverty." He was the first saint to receive the stigmata.

Saint Francis of Assisi was one of the most famous Christian saints; possibly the most attractive and doubtlessly the most popular among not only non-Catholics but also atheists.

Nicholas Roerich.
Saint Francis of Assisi

For 800 years, the personality of Saint Francis of Assisi had been of interest to people of most diverse views: church hierarchs and philosophers, kings and revolutionaries. He was seen as a founder of subjectivism and individualism, a precursor of the Renaissance, a reformer, a socialist, a first hippy, a fighter for ecology, and a romantic hero. Surprisingly enough, the life of Francis of Assisi was nothing but an exact following of the ideal of Christianity and imitating Christ.

People believe that it was Saint Francis of Assisi who brought the spirit of happiness into gloomy austere Christianity of the Middle Ages. However, this is not entirely true — the joy and happiness of gratitude to the Creator, the joy and happiness of Resurrection were inherent features of Christianity. In Eastern Christianity, Clement of Alexandria and John Chrysostom were the propagators of happiness; in Western Christianity, it was Saint Benedict. Francis of Assisi did not invent anything that could be considered a discovery in Christianity; however, without him Christianity would not become as attractive to millions of believers as it is today.

Francis (Francesco) Bernardone was born in 1181 (or 1182) in Assisi to the family of a textile merchant. Francesco had a carefree and cheerful childhood and youth. When he was twenty-four he heard a voice of Christ in the church of St. Damian. Christ called him to service — at least this is what his hagiographers say. As a young man, Francesco left his family and started living in poverty, taking care of lepers and restoring desolate churches. On February 24, 1209, on the day of St. Matthew, during mass, he had a revelation that his mission was to follow the Gospel word for word; so the lonely hermit became a traveling preacher. He gained some companions. He gave them the regulations of evangelical life, of which Pope Innocent III approved in 1210. Thus, in medieval Europe, another cloistral order appeared. Saint Francis preached, performed miracles like many other Christian saints, and passed away suffering from the incipient disregard of his regulations.

Why then was he outstanding and what brought the volunteering pauper from Assisi this glory? Saint Francis was a founder of proactive monasticism – missionary activity; his spirituality gave meaning to the art of the early Italian Renaissance, especially to the art of Giotto. His "Hymn the Sun" became the first poem in the Italian language, which gave a push to the development of poetry in national languages and inspired great Dante. However, probably the most important and attractive feature about Saint Francis was the atmosphere of love, kindness, and simplicity which he was able to maintain around him in his lifetime and which was well conveyed by his contemporaries in the hagiography preserved to the present day, especially, in "Flowerets of Saint Francis."[7]

God opened to Saint Francis the divine presence in the "brother-Sun" and in the "sister-Moon" and rewarded him for his loyalty to the stigmata of crucified Jesus. Saint Frances's prayer is known around the world. People of all religions chant it:

Lord, make me an instrument of thy peace.
Where there is hatred, let me sow love;
Where there is injury, pardon;
Where there is doubt, faith;
Where there is despair, hope;
Where there is darkness, light;
Where there is sadness, joy.

O Divine Master, grant that I may not so much seek
To be consoled as to console,
To be understood as to understand,

---

[7] "Flowerets of Saint Francis of Assisi"

To be loved as to love;
For it is in giving that we receive;
It is in pardoning that we are pardoned;
It is in dying to self that we are born to eternal life.

Shah Jahan (1592-1666) was another incarnation of Kuthumi. Shah Jahan was an Indian emperor from the dynasty of the Mughals. After his father Jahangir's death, Shah Jahan inherited the throne and partly restored the noble ethics of his grandfather — Akbar the Great. During his reign, the greatness of the Mughals reached its apogee and India witnessed a rapid growth in art and architecture. The Taj Mahal, erected in the capital of India, Agra, became an example of this growth. Shah Jahan spent funds from the state treasury on music, painting, and building majestic monuments — mosques and public buildings around India, some of which have survived to the present day.

The famous Taj Mahal — "the wonder of wonders, the last miracle of the world" — was built as a tomb for Shah Jahan's beloved wife Mumtaz Mahal. She ruled together with her husband almost on equal terms and died in labor of their fourteenth child in 1631. Erecting the monument as beautiful as his wife, Shah Jahan spared no expense. The monument is a symbol of Love and immortalizes the Emperor's imperishable life to Mumtaz Mahal.

This book presents to reader's attention Messages of the Master Kuthumi, transmitted from 2005 to 2013. The Messages address new aspects of the Law of Karma, provide a new understanding of the structure and evolution of man and the Universe and of the purpose and meaning of Existence.

From the Editor

You must aspire to control your thoughts and feelings

March 24, 2005

I AM Kuthumi. I have come!

I have come to use this opportunity and to talk to you.

You know me as a Master Psychologist. You also know me as the person who incarnated together with El Morya to found the Theosophical Society and to give mankind the knowledge previously hidden from it.

You know me as a Teacher of the World, sharing this position with beloved Jesus.

You know my incarnations as Pythagoras and Shah Jahan.

You know much about me. I am an open Master.

I am the Master who aspires to contact non-ascended mankind, and I work with many of you.

We have given you enough knowledge in the course of the last 150 years. And we will continue to give new knowledge to those who are ready to understand it. But first you are to master some of the lessons we gave in the past.

You should agree that although mankind has always aspired to receive this knowledge, for some reason mankind reluctantly applies the received knowledge in practice.

It is expedient to give new knowledge only if the older material has already been mastered. Otherwise you simply will not be able to take in the new one.

Your consciousness is like a kind of vessel. When a person is incarnated, his consciousness is limited. Due to the gift of free will, you decide what to fill the vessel of your consciousness with.

When it happens that a disciple is ready to assimilate a certain amount of knowledge, but his consciousness does not have the necessary aspiration and direction, in this case, he prefers to fill the vessel of his consciousness with everything he meets in the external world — that is, everything that he reads in the newspapers, watches on TV, or listens to on the radio.

Such an omnivorous way of receiving information is permitted until a certain moment — but only until a certain moment.

26

Therefore, if a person makes no effort to limit the information stream coming into his external consciousness from the physical world, he will fill his consciousness with a mass of unnecessary things, and when the cosmic moment comes for receiving the true knowledge, because the Heavens decide to give this knowledge to non-ascended mankind, the consciousness of such an individual will be simply unable to master anything new.

What is worse, such an individual is not able to navigate in all this chaos of information contained in his consciousness. For him, the information obtained from the press has the same importance as the information received from the Dictations of the Ascended Masters.

Part of this information rubbish is moved to the subconscious and settles there. Sometimes, when a monster of any internal psychological problem unites with similar vibrations contained in the so-called mass media, the result is manifested in the external behavior of a person and is so unpredictable and goes beyond all reasonable bounds, so that nobody can explain his behavior and no psychologist can help him to solve this unexpected psychological problem.

However, you create all your problems your-selves. You do it exactly at the moment when you place into the vessel of your consciousness all the information you receive in life, without thinking about the consequences. You have already been told repeatedly through this Messenger that 90 percent of the information surrounding you in your world is false and you do not need it for your evolution as spiritual beings.

That is why I suggest that you begin by limiting your omnivorous nature. You should not rely too much on any information that comes to you from the external world.

First, you should aspire to control your thoughts and feelings.

Just spare some ten to fifteen minutes a day for yourselves, when nothing diverts your attention. You may do this before going to bed. Try to discover what you are thinking about. Examine your thoughts closely. Scrutinize them. Imagine that your thoughts are fish in the aquarium. Now one thought swims up to you. Examine it. What is this thought connected with? If this thought ties you down to this world or makes you concentrate on the surrounding world, let it go. You do not need it for your spiritual growth.

Then closely examine your second thought and the next one.

Your consciousness is filled with so many thoughts that are nothing else but energy, attracted by you from outside and consonant with the energy of your emotional and mental bodies.

As you analyze what you are thinking about at such a moment, you can also analyze all your thoughts of the passing day.

And you will understand that your consciousness is so busy processing the unnecessary information that you simply lack enough strength of your consciousness to start processing the information that is really useful for your evolution.

That is why the most important task for you is to come to a decision that you will no longer fill your consciousness with unnecessary information from the surrounding physical world.

Then you will possibly decide to practice some kind of meditation that will help you free yourself from thoughts that tie you down to this world.

The aim of any meditation practice, if it is true, is to reach a state of being without thoughts.

And when you manage to keep this state for a long enough time, you will be able to gain access to the true information that is really necessary for your spiritual evolution.

The time has come when the mental field of the planet must be purified. Only when you empty a saucepan can you fill it with the things necessary for you at present.

I suggest that you should seriously revise your attitude to thoughtlessly allowing your consciousness to be under the influence of different information streams in your world.

You should have understood from these Dictations that your world contains 90 percent of needless information. Become free from this needless information and you will gain access to the information that is really necessary for you.

The same can be said about your feelings.

Analyze your feelings during the day. You do not need to look at other people. I know that people — especially people from Russia — are constantly in a state close to depression. Watch your feelings during the day. How often do you feel love, joy, and experience inexplicable high spirits? How many times have you stopped in the street to admire the trees or clouds? How often do you go out to be in nature?

Your emotions, as well as your thoughts, are under the influence of Earth's general information field. And this field prevents any images and ideas of the higher octaves from penetrating your dense physical world.

Mankind keeps itself under a solid net of its own imperfect thoughts and feelings, and it was its own will to be driven there.

Now you should start to clear out the rubbish heaps of your imperfect thoughts and feelings.

Your mass media tune into the average level of human consciousness. That is why they prevent you from entering a higher level of your consciousness. Give up using information surrogates, and then the mass media, pushed by competitive struggle, will start adapting to your level of consciousness.

This world is only a reflection of your consciousness. If you change your consciousness, then you will be able to attract to yourselves more perfect manifestations from the higher world.

And then there will be a precipitation of perfect patterns, which have already been prepared for you long ago by the most advanced minds of humanity and are waiting for you to let this perfection descend into your world.

The aim of my talk today is to remind you that you are responsible for everything happening on Earth.

Therefore, do not be lazy and let no grass grow under your feet; start transforming your consciousness right now.

I AM Kuthumi, with love to you.

A Teaching on twin flames

April 26, 2005

I AM Kuthumi, having come to you through this Messenger. I have come to give you a new Teaching about twin flames, different from the Teaching that was given to you before.

You know that every man and every woman embodied on Earth is endowed with both masculine and feminine side. As a matter of fact, you are asexual in your highest aspect and you are androgynous in your Higher bodies. Only in the course of the condensing and differentiating of the matter, you first acquire your physical body and after that the signs of this or that sex. The previous conception was erroneous because you thought that somewhere outside of you there was a part of you that had been separated from you at a certain stage of evolution.

In fact, if we touch upon the history of the evolution of your souls, the white-fire core of your being, or your I AM Presence, the immortal particle of God inside of you has never been divided into two parts representing masculine and feminine aspects. It was a misconception that we allowed in order to reveal this idea to you at a certain stage of your evolution. Now, a new period has come, and we can give you another view on the evolution of your soul, slightly different from the previous one.

Thus, your Higher body has never been divided into masculine and feminine polarity. Then where is the origin of the ideas about twin flames and of all these beautiful legends about the search for one's second half and acquiring unity through the official marriage between twin flames?

Let me explain. Your soul, as well as your Higher body, has no sex. They are genderless. Only your physical body has a sex, and it has acquired its sexual signs only during a relatively recent stage of evolution, several million years ago.

Before the appearance of sexual division, the process of procreation was absolutely different. But we will not become absorbed in this now.

So, where did the idea of your second half and the happiness connected with it originate?

At a certain stage of evolution, you acquired your Higher body, which has received different names in different religious systems. This is your Christ Self, or Higher Self, or the Highest Manas.

You may have understood from these Dictations that your Higher Self was given to you as an emanation of the higher spiritual beings who granted a particle of themselves to you. This was necessary at a certain stage of human evolution. A person had to receive a conductor inside of himself, which by following the instructions you would be able to acquire the feeling of unity with God and the entire creation that you lack so much.

Beloved Jesus, when in incarnation, gave a Teaching of the unity of the soul. You remember the parable about a bridegroom, and you remember the mention of the bride who prepared herself for the arrival of the bridegroom. This is the Teaching on the twin flames given by Jesus, but it has another meaning, a more correct one. The unity with your twin flame is your union with your Higher part.

A new stage of cosmic evolution is approaching, and this stage is already not far off, when each of you will have to find the unity with your twin flame, with your Christ Self.

The union of the twin flames is a ritual in which the vibrations of your lower bodies or soul become harmonious with your Higher body, your Christ Self.

Since by this moment, you will have completely purified your lower bodies, energy will freely circulate through your bodies, washing your bodies.

The ecstasy of unity that you experience when reuniting with the Higher part of yourself raises you to the apex of such other-worldly bliss that cannot be compared with the unity between a man and a woman in the physical plane.

Oh, beloved, God has many more secrets and mysteries that will be revealed to you in due time. Today I have probably blighted in your minds a beautiful legend about twin flames that was close to the heart of everybody who managed to know this Teaching given through the previous Messenger. But sooner or later you have to part with children's fairy tales and become adults.

When being in the mature state of consciousness, it is always pleasant to encounter miracles in your life, the description of which you did not meet even in the best fairy tales. This is because the Divine Reality and the recognition of the Divine Reality cannot be compared with the boldest fantasies of the story tellers who are nevertheless interpreting the Divine Truth in accordance with their human consciousness.

Now, beloved, I will dwell upon one more topic that can amaze you. Since in those remote times every Being of Light endowed many lifestreams with its particle, the Christ Self of many of you is of the same nature and belongs to the same Being of Light that endowed you with its particle.

When you reach the state of unity with your Higher part and other people also reach the unity with their Higher part, you become united with each other. You feel unity with everyone. And instead of one twin flame, you experience unity with millions of twin flames that have a common nature with your Christ Self.

However, there is another aspect of the twin flames legend, and this aspect is connected with an even earlier stage of cosmic evolution. Once upon a time, at the dawn of the creation of this Universe, a division into masculine and feminine polarity occurred, and this division served as a starting point for the Universe to become manifested. It was the point from where the whole creation started to be manifested. That is why, when in the course of your evolution you and your Universe return to that point again, both masculine and feminine polarities in this Universe will disappear. But this will take place in infinitely remote times by human standards.

Now your consciousness cannot accommodate many cosmic Truths. I do not think it is my task to reveal to you all the Truths, even as I see them from my Ascended state of consciousness.

For the present I have told you enough.

As a consolation, I can tell you that those individuals who have a Christ Self of the same nature as my Christ Self are to some extent my twin flames. That is why, accepting your Christ Self, which is by right your twin flame, you have several millions more twin flames embodied now that have a common nature with you at the level of Christ Self.

This can either encourage or disappoint some of you.

However, it is impossible to stop the process of the comprehension of the Divine Truth. This process will continue and the perpetual revelation will go on. Whether you like it or not, the process of the evolution of your consciousness cannot be stopped, but if you resist the progress, then think about whether you act in accordance with the Divine Law.

In today's talk, I have shown you your twin flame that is always with you, patiently waiting for you to stop being carried away by the illusion of this world and fasten your eyes on it. Your twin flame wishes to communicate with you; it is waiting for you. And there is no person in this world that is closer to you and with whom you can share all your secrets and from whom you can receive reliable advice.

I lapse into silence to give you an opportunity to master the unexpected information given in today's talk.

I AM Kuthumi, and I have a common nature with many of you at the level of Christ Self.

We come to awaken your Divinity

May 8, 2005

I AM Kuthumi, having come to you through this Messenger again.

I have come to give you some clarification relating to the Teaching I gave a few days ago.[8] This is the Teaching on twin flames.

Many of you did not expect to hear such an interpretation of this Teaching in the form that I gave.

However, sooner or later your conception of yourselves and of your souls should be broadened.

In reality, you are absolutely different from the image of yourselves that you have created in your external consciousness. And your might is unlimited.

---

[8] Refer to the Dictation "A Teaching on twin flames," Beloved Kuthumi, April 26, 2005 in *Words of Wisdom Volume I.*

The potential to be God is lies within you, within each of you.

As a matter of fact, you are Gods. And your task is to gradually master your Divinity and to let Divinity enter your external consciousness.

Do believe that you are not people going to play the role of Gods; you are Gods who have come temporarily to play the role of people.

Your Divinity is hidden from your external consciousness, and your abilities are asleep within you until you completely fulfill your task in this world.

Millions of years ago, the seeds of your souls sowed the planets that were appearing at that time. Your immortal particle, your monad, has passed through all stages and all levels of the development of the material Universe in its evolution.

You were a stone, you were a plant, you were an insect, you were a representative of the lower animal kingdom, and you were the higher animals. You have passed through all these stages of evolution. You have passed them not only on this planet but on other planets as well.

All this took billions of terrestrial years.

The particle of God that constitutes your foundation was gradually being enriched with the experiences of your entire existence in the material Universe.

It looks as if you have come to work at a plant in a large company. You know that you are to become the director of this plant in due course. But in order to be a good leader you have decided to pass through all the stages and steps of the career ladder beginning from that of a basic worker through that of a leader of the lower and medium levels, to that of the director.

When passing through all the stages of your work at the plant, you acquire grains of knowledge and experience shared with you by the people who have already gained work experience and mastered all the skills of their profession.

Imagine that you have come to the design department, and the leader of this department spends many hours with you, teaching you all the intricacies of the design business and the skills that he has mastered over long years of his work in his position.

To draw an analogy with your position as people on Earth, at a certain stage of your evolution you receive an inner mentor which is your Christ Self, belonging to the higher beings that have already passed the human stage of evolution many millions of years ago. And this highly evolved being grants you a particle that becomes your mentor and your closest and best friend.

At the same time, you are endowed with reason, the intelligence that differentiates humans from animals and is rightfully your tempter. It is so because after being endowed with reason and with free will at the same time, a person can use his reason both to maintain his life in the physical world and to advance on the path of evolution and perfection of his self in God.

Your reason is what sets you apart from animals, and at the same time, in accordance with your free will, you are allowed to use your reason just to get merely animal pleasures of life and to surround yourselves with all the pleasures of the physical world that come to your mind.

To return to the analogy of your internship in the design department, you start using the knowledge you have gained in the sphere of construction in order to design something that will enable you to create a machine that will fulfill all your wishes. And imagine that you start designing this machine and begin to use all the resources of the entire design department and then the capacity of the whole plant for that.

Sooner or later your actions will be stopped because your activity does not correspond to the purpose for which this plant was built.

You will have to either submit to the purpose for which you were invited to work or leave the precincts of the company where you have started your work.

Exactly in the same way, you are faced with the task at the current stage of your evolution: either to give up satisfying your irrepressible desires in the physical world and concentrate on the task for which your immortal particle has come to this world in order to pass the necessary internship, or you will have to leave the precincts of this world because your interests have come into conflict with the plan for this Universe, and you must be stopped.

The difference is that there is no other plant in this Universe where you can find a job.

You were given your mind at a certain stage of evolutionary development, and your task during all this enormous historical period of human development has been to master your mind and to place its mere carnal and animal inclinations under the command of the Divine guidance.

The time has come when you must give up the carnal part of your mind and completely submit yourselves to the Divine reason. Both are present within you. You only have to differentiate one from another in your consciousness and voluntarily give up everything that can obstruct you in the next stage of your evolution when you are to pass from animal-man to God-man.

At this stage you will need your friend and mentor, your Christ Self, who is patiently waiting for you to finally pay attention to him and to be able to start studying under his immediate guidance.

It is time to part with your children's toys, filling your material world, and fix your eyes on the real world.

Your Christ Self is exactly the part of you with which you must unite in your consciousness in the near future. This is your authentic twin flame, the bridegroom of your soul.

You see how simple everything is, beloved.

The Teaching of God is a very simple Teaching in fact. And all the difficulty of the comprehension of this Teaching is that you must perceive with your external mind the things that do not belong to your world. You can do this only by using your Divine abilities that are present within you but are dormant in most of humanity.

We come to awaken your dormant abilities. We come to awaken your Divinity. The time has come for you to voluntarily submit yourselves to the Higher Reason, manifesting the Higher Will within you.

I have been glad to give you this additional clarification regarding the current stage of the evolution of your soul.

I AM Kuthumi, and I AM always with you on your Path.

Try to keep the state of inner peace and harmony during most of the day

May 19, 2005

I AM Kuthumi, having come to you again. I have come today to give you a small Teaching which perhaps may seem unexpected to you, but I would still like you to carefully familiarize yourselves with everything that I consider necessary to bring to your consciousness at this stage.

As you know, the event that took place at the end of last year — an earthquake and a tsunami — was entirely caused by the imperfect consciousness of mankind.

With surprising persistence, humanity continues to give birth to monstrous masses of negative energies that have wrapped the entire globe with a thick envelope. This envelope prevents the penetration of the renewal energies. In other words, a tension has been created between the forces that strive to keep the existing state on the planet and the forces striving to contribute to the implementation of the evolutionary plan for planet Earth.

On the one hand, you witness the constant and steady rise of the vibrations of the planet. On the other hand, an enormous amount of negative energy is still produced with the help of mass consciousness and the old stereotypes deeply ingrained in the consciousness of people. Where does the negative energy come from?

All the energy in this Universe is concentrated in only one source, and that is the Divine energy. This energy comes to you along the crystal string, and you use this energy of your own free will. If you waste this energy to satisfy any of your egoistic strivings or to maintain negative thoughts, qualities, or persistent bad habits, then it means that you vote for the obsolete way of living. You direct your energy to strengthen the masses of negative energy on this planet.

Therefore, when the positive energy of change meets with the negative energy produced by humanity, it is like a clash of two clouds with different charges. You know what happens when such clouds collide. You can observe thunder and lightning. Something similar is taking place on planet Earth at present. When two masses of energies with opposite potential clash, various disasters happen — for example, natural calamities and hurricanes.

It may seem to you that the natural elements are blind and uncontrollable. However, this is not quite true. As a rule, we manage to localize the masses of emerging negative energy at the places where they appear. That is why the areas that contribute to the production of the negative energetic masses with their consciousness suffer from the natural calamities.

Beloved, it is time to part with the point of view that you can commit sins, act in improper ways, think and feel in ways unpleasing to God during most of the day, and then after that you can sit down, pray, and transmute the karma that you and your loved ones have created.

There is no doubt that the benefits of prayers are unquestionable, undeniable, and indisputable. The effectiveness of prayers is beyond discussion. But it is not enough just to pray in this situation, beloved.

What is the point of first producing negative energetic masses and then fighting against them?

It is time for you to approach everything you do during the day consciously. You should constantly control your thoughts and feelings. Any negative thought in your consciousness must be nipped in the bud. Protect yourself from everything that contributes to the existence of negative thoughts and feelings in your consciousness.

Pay special attention to your children. Do not leave them alone during most of the day. Remember that the fruit that you will get literally in a few years will depend on the direction you show your children at the beginning of their lives and on the knowledge that you give them about the laws operating in this Universe, for your children will grow up and will be able to take responsibilities upon themselves and to serve for the benefit of the evolution of Earth. Each of you is responsible for the future of this planet and for the unfolding of the events in the coming months.

Remember that the tension, which was defused by the cataclysm in the south of Asia at the end of last year, is increasing again. As a matter of fact, with every negative action and every negative thought and feeling, you tirelessly draw a new cataclysm nearer.

Try to keep the state of inner peace and harmony during most of the day. Do not forget that other people live next to you. If you live in a big city, during the day your aura comes into contact with the auras of thousands of people. When you manage to keep a harmonious state within yourself, you literally infect with this state thousands of people with whose auras you come into contact during the day.

Exactly the same effect occurs when you meet a person who is like a thundercloud and seeking someone to ease his tension and to vent his anger. But in this case you are infected with the negative energies of this person.

Protect your inner world against the intrusion of negative energies. Take special care of your children.

You can say that nothing depends on you and that your government is to be blamed for everything because it does not take proper care of you and does not allow you to enjoy a decent way of life.

Allow me to disagree with you. All things in this world are drawn to each other by their vibrations, and you have exactly the government that can exist only because the majority of the population considers it possible to tolerate this government and its policies.

You constantly exchange energies with thousands of people, and thus you constantly exchange karma with them. How do you think the karma of a family is manifested, the karma of the city, the karma of the country, or the planetary karma? Imagine a person who is completely free from his personal karma. What do you think will happen to this person next? Will he ascend?

It is quite probable that such a person can ascend. But let me assure you that a person who has become free from his personal karma acquires a completely different expanded consciousness. He rises up to another higher level in his consciousness and understands that it is impossible to save only his own soul. Actually, everything is God, and at this new level of consciousness the person feels the unity of all the living much more deeply. Such a person is most likely to stay in embodiment regardless of whether his external consciousness is aware of his decision or not. Such a person continues to live in the world of his choice. Every day he draws the negative energies of the people around him into his aura and transmutes these energies. Such a person is like a sponge. As soon as he comes in contact with the auras of people saturated with too much negative energy, he takes a part of this energy upon himself and neutralizes it. A phenomenon occurs that you call the transmutation of the karma of a city, a country, or a planet.

Therefore, very much depends on each of you, beloved, on your ability to keep harmony and balance, in spite of any surrounding circumstances. If you feel depression, lack of joy, causeless melancholy, then it means that you have most likely come under the influence of a large mass of negative energy. You have loaded your aura so heavily that you will need some time to be alone or in nature to restore your inner peace and balance.

Learn to recognize your inner state and the reasons for disharmony in your consciousness.

When you reach a certain level of consciousness that allows you to take upon yourself the karma of a city, a country, or the planet and to transmute this karma, you serve constantly, 24 hours a day.

This is a vital service, beloved. Today I have given these recommendations for you in the hope of explaining the mechanism of such a service to those of you who are already providing this vital service to the world. And when you are now aware of your service, you will be able to take timely measures for the restoration of your vibrations and energies. Listen carefully to your body, and when you are overcome with depression, find a way to restore your inner harmony and peace. For some of you it can be meditation; for others it can be a prayer, a stroll in nature, listening to relaxing music, or playing with children.

Do not allow yourself to be in the negative state of consciousness for a long time. Suppress all the negative vibrations within you as soon as they arise. Do not let them take hold of your being.

And remember that you always have an opportunity to ask the Ascended Hosts for help as a last resort. We will render to our devoted servants all the help that the Cosmic Law will allow us.

I AM Kuthumi, your brother.

A Teaching on karma

May 31, 2005

I AM Kuthumi, having come to you through this Messenger again.

I have come to give you a small Teaching and to consolidate the knowledge that has already been given in previous Dictations. The Hosts of Light are invisibly present among you and try to make use of every chance to be present in your world as soon as a gap is created, a space of pure vibrations that allows us to do this.

Our worlds enrich each other reciprocally. Do not think of your world as the devil incarnate.

Yes, the situation in your world is rather deplorable today, but this will not last forever. Both the purification of your world and inevitably the subsequent rise of the vibrations of the physical plane, are necessary conditions for the further evolutionary progress of humanity.

Since your karma is very large and it consists of the karma of each individual and the entire planet, this hardened energy, solidified as karma, creates your dense world.

When karma is worked off through the rise of human consciousness, the rejection of wrong actions, and maintaining the right Divine accord of thoughts and feelings, the physical plane gradually becomes less and less dense until it disappears altogether. Nevertheless, long before the physical plane of planet Earth disappears, life will move from this plane to the higher ones. These planes are very close to you at present, especially the astral and the mental planes. You can sit motionless at home or even at work while at the same time your mental or emotional body can wander around the mental and the astral planes. These journeys can even reach your external consciousness and either be realized by your outer mind or not.

You leave your body and travel to the astral plane every night. Your external consciousness does not always realize where you traveled and whom you met at night. There are some individuals capable of remembering their dreams and even of making conscious journeys in their dreams in order to meet the people that they want to meet.

Such an activity, as well as any other activity typical of your world, may be used both for good and for evil aims. Everything depends on the aim of the person making astral journeys and on the motives a person is guided by — whether he wishes to influence the individuals whom he meets for his own mercenary aims or he does this for the benefit of the planet.

The journeys out of the body in your less dense bodies are quite natural. These journeys take place independently whether you realize it with your outer consciousness or not.

Nonetheless, I must warn you that if you use a conscious journey to the astral plane in order to influence some person or even to harm someone, then your actions entail the same karma as if you performed them in the physical plane with full consciousness in broad daylight.

If your external consciousness does not understand what you are doing in the astral plane, this will not free you from the karmic responsibility for your actions.

I will tell you more. Many individuals create much more karma in their dreams than during the waking state of consciousness. Similarly, when you are at home and make an unconscious journey to the astral or mental plane while your thoughts and feelings are aimed against any person, you create karma.

If you play mental images of some vindictive or sexual scenes through your consciousness, you create the same karma as if you really performed all these actions in the physical plane.

That is why we are never tired of saying to you again and again that you must constantly control your thoughts and feelings. During your night sleep you are drawn to those layers of the astral plane with the quality of vibrations that corresponds to your thoughts before going to sleep. If before going to bed you watched a horror film or spent time in drunken company, then you will be drawn to those layers of the astral plane where you will continue your evening entertainment. In this case you create the same karma as if you were doing all this on the physical plane.

That is why your mood during the day and especially before going to bed is very important.

The best thing is to pray or if you are not used to praying before sleep, then at least to listen to soft music or have a stroll in nature. It would also be useful to read a good fairy tale to your children before sleep.

And, of course, do not forget before going to bed to ask the angels to accompany you to the etheric octaves of Light where the sacred retreats of the Brotherhood are located.

You can even specify precisely which of the Masters you would like to meet during your night sleep and frame a question that you would like to get the answer to.

If you ask me a specific question before going to sleep, then the first thing you should do in the morning is to concentrate and remember the answer given by me during your sleep.

As a rule, I give answers to everyone who reaches me in my retreat and asks me questions during his night sleep. It depends only on you to recall this answer and to write it down immediately after awakening.

You see how differently you can spend time during your night sleep. And it is up to you to make a choice as to how to use your night sleep. You literally program yourselves before going to sleep for the actions that you perform during your night sleep.

Therefore, I repeat again and again: You must control your thoughts and feelings constantly, every minute. Always remember that if the situations that you bottle up in your mind are subject to karmic punishment, then you create karma by just thinking about them.

In this case, the technique for creating karma is the following: The Divine Energy, entering your four lower bodies from the Divine world along the crystal string, is tinted by your thoughts and feelings. If your thoughts are imperfect, then you qualify the Divine Energy falsely.

It is very important to control the state of your consciousness at every moment. Your consciousness is so mobile that we never cease to marvel at your ability to create so much karma even during prayer.

That is why you are told about the practice of meditation as one of the possible ways to calm your mind.

Only if you manage to calm all your fussy thoughts and feelings and reach complete peace of your mind, then you become able to ascend to the higher etheric octaves of Light and stay there for a long time. You become able to meet with the Masters, to talk with them, and to walk with them around the etheric octaves of Light.

For that reason, to be able to indirectly judge the level of your spiritual merits, set the alarm clock so that it can give you a signal every hour. When you hear the alarm, try to recall what you were thinking about at that moment.

If at that time you were thinking about some elevated and spiritual things, then you can mark it as figure 1 on a piece of paper or in your memory. If your thoughts were imperfect, mark it as 0.

It is enough to catch your thoughts ten times a day according to this technique. Sum up all of the figure 1s, append a 0 to them and you will see the approximate percentage of the karma worked off by you.

For example, if six out of ten your thoughts could be characterized as elevated, the percentage of the worked off karma is approximately 60 percent.

It is not strange if one day you record 10 percent as the amount of the worked off karma and the next day the result is 70 percent. In fact, your karma changes during the day. Karma is energy, and if you spend most of the day in nature and do not communicate with anybody, then the percentage of the worked-off karma will be the most approximate to your natural index, achieved by you at this stage of your development. If you come into contact with thousands of people during the day, then you exchange energy with them every time you touch their auras or during conversations and teamwork. Consequently, you exchange karma every time you come in contact with people during the day.

That is why all the venerable elders, prophets, and yogis preferred a secluded way of life and did not associate with people.

Thus, it is impossible for you not to carry the karma of your family, your city, and your planet while you live on Earth.

The humans of Earth are very interrelated by their karma. It takes a high level of spiritual achievement to acquire the ability to become independent of the karma of the people around you.

Do not forget that the Law of Likeness acts in your world. You are drawn to the people and situations in order to work off your karma.

When a Buddha walks on the Earth, no karmic situation can affect him. He steps on Earth without being noticed by anybody, and no negative energies can cling to him. However, in order for a Buddha to come to your world, he must first take imperfection or karma upon himself. It is like a diver who takes a stone in his hands before making a dive.

For that reason, you are strongly advised not to judge anyone. You never can say whether it is a Buddha or the lowest sinner standing in front of you, because both of them can be burdened with similar karma at times. But if one of them takes upon himself the karma of humanity intentionally, feeling compassion for people and wishing to help them, the other burdens himself with this karma only because of his ignorance.

Today I have touched on some of the topics that were already known to you. Together we have examined many questions from a new angle. The questions of karma are very complex and I raise my hat to the members of the Karmic Board, because

I realize how considerable the difficulties are that they encounter in their work.

I AM Kuthumi.

A Teaching on good Karma

June 6, 2005

I AM Kuthumi, having come to you again. The purpose of my coming today is to acquaint you with one more viewpoint on the structure of the world. When contacting our reality, your sensations do not always reflect the real state of affairs. You are used to grounding your perception of the world according to your sensory organs, and you completely trust your sensory organs. And really, why in the world should you believe in something you do not see and why should you act in accordance with our recommendations when you do not even have an opportunity to meet with us directly without the help of this Messenger?

However, this is a question of your faith. You either believe that the world around you is not the entire Creation and that the entire Creation is actually much larger, or you do not believe it.

You cannot start knowing something that you do not believe in. You cannot sense the things that you know could not exist. However, as soon as you begin to believe in the real world of God that is invisible and not perceived by your sensory organs but is not less real because of that, you almost immediately start conceptualizing our world.

The Higher worlds contact you and you are constantly coming into contact with the Higher worlds. You just do not pay attention to our reality. But our communication with each of you is not only possible, but it is in progress all the time. And the same way as you do not notice radio waves penetrating you constantly, the vibrations of our world come into contact with you all the time and you do not perceive them. If you properly prepare your temple and above all, you believe in the reality of our world, then you will inevitably be able to perceive our world.

Imagine that I have an opportunity to talk to you. I come to you and sit in front of you. You do not see me. You do not see me for two reasons. The first reason is that you do not expect me to come, and within your consciousness you are not ready for my arrival. The second reason is that you do not perceive my presence with your physical sensory organs.

Which of the two reasons separating us is the most essential and difficult to overcome?

I will tell you that it is the first one. When your consciousness is ready to contact the Higher worlds and to communicate with the Ascended Hosts, you will start your communication regardless of whether your sensory organs perceive this communication or not.

Your body has untapped, dormant abilities that enable you to hear without listening, to see without looking, to know and to get information almost immediately without the help of thoughts and words and without the help of your physical sensory organs.

This seems to be fantastic to you, but if you turn to the history of the greatest inventions and discoveries, you will come across an amazing regularity. All these inventions and discoveries burst upon the mind of their inventors out of nowhere. A person would tune in to a certain wave of thoughts associated with some branch of human activity, and suddenly receive insights in the form of knowledge that appeared in his head out of nowhere.

Certainly, it is very difficult to give an idea to a person who has no knowledge, for example, in the field of computer programing about the essence of invention in the field of modern knowledge such as the Internet or the contemporary means of communication. But for a person who has this knowledge, it will not be difficult to receive the new information coming into his external consciousness and connected with the subject of his activity.

Many things like that take place completely spontaneously. And a person who has discovered an invention usually does not even think about the mechanism of how the idea for the invention crossed his mind.

The same may be said about you. Having an idea of the Ascended Hosts, you can receive information from us that suddenly appears in your head and, even without knowing how it happens, you will be able to be guided by this information in your activities.

If you think carefully, each of you will certainly recollect a few examples of how miraculously you managed to find some lost things, or to get an idea of how to behave in a difficult situation, or to obtain an utterly miraculous solution to an intricate task that you were facing in your life.

All these miracles are the interference of the Higher plane in your life. And you receive the realization of these miraculous opportunities due to either your Higher Self or the intervention of the Ascended Hosts.

The complexity is in the fact that the time passes differently in our worlds. That is why the moment of your request may not coincide with the moment when you receive the thing requested. It is natural that your requests can be satisfied only if you possess enough good karma to fulfill your requests.

It seems unreasonable for a practical person to waste efforts on doing some good things absolutely disinterestedly without a backward glance and without looking forward to getting a reward for his good deed in the near future.

But the reason for your indecisiveness and unwillingness to perform good deeds selflessly is again your disbelief in the Divine Law.

You suppose that if you donate to a church, to an orphanage, or to any charitable organization, then you must immediately receive from God a multiplication of the money you spend on charity.

Beloved, everything depends on the motive that is the basis of your decision to donate. If you sacrifice in order to receive something in return, or if you think that God will forget about the sin you committed, or if you make your donation in order to show everybody your generosity, then this sacrifice will not create good karma for you.

You must just perform good deeds without thinking about the consequences and the benefits that this sacrifice can bring to you in the future.

In this case you really create good karma. And this good karma of yours can help you when you are in a difficult situation and call to God and ask Him for help.

God will help you. It is impossible for God not to help you. But for this help, the energy of your good karma in your causal body will be used.

If you do not have enough good karma at the moment of your request, you will not receive the help you need and ask for.

You receive exactly what you give to the world. And if you have not performed at least one good deed during all your life and during all your previous lives, then why do you think God will respond to your request when you are in need?

For that reason, if I were you in embodiment, I would funnel all my energies and put all my cash assets into helping those living beings that need my help. In this case your good deeds will be accumulated in the form of energy in your causal body. It is similar to when you save money for a rainy day. The difference is only in that you save your money in the form of energy in another world. And there is no more reliable place in your world for keeping this energy and your savings.

This energy of yours can always be requested by you through your appeal to God at a moment when you need Divine help.

Consequently, when you call to God and say, "Help me, Lord!" and if at that moment there is not enough energy stored in your depository in Heaven to help you, then do not hold a grievance against God; hold it as a grievance against yourself because it was you who did not care about yourself and have not stocked the necessary amount of good karma in order to create a reserve of your merits in Heaven.

Today I have given you a very important Teaching on good karma. I hope that all of you will be able to apply this Teaching in practice. Just imagine how good it could be for you if you took this Teaching as a guideline in your life, and how wonderful it would be if all people on Earth made a dash to create good karma. Each of you would be able to receive all the necessary help from the people who would literally be running around the Earth in search of those who are in need of their help. Besides, if you created the necessary amount of good karma, you could always appeal to God for help and receive help.

I wish you to succeed in your practice of creating good karma. May you create only good karma in the future and for the rest of your life.

I AM Kuthumi.

There is a section of the Path that you will not be able to overcome alone without a guide

June 7, 2005

I AM Kuthumi, having come to you again.

I have come to continue teaching you. As you know, we are trying to do everything we can to ensure that all the knowledge you receive from these Dictations is easily mastered by you and without causing resentment.

The process of teaching you is akin to the process of feeding little children. We select your food carefully and make sure that you do not overeat or remain hungry.

The main responsibility of a Teacher is to care about his disciples. However, at times our care for your souls is felt by you as a punishment or an attempt upon your independence.

Indeed, when you set your mind on entering the Path, instead of receiving the expected comfort and the constant feeling of bliss and harmony, you start facing completely obscure things that require additional explanation on our part. As soon as we see that a disciple is ready and his determination to follow the Path reaches a certain level, we take this disciple under our intensive tutorship. From this moment, the disciple can no longer say that he can enjoy his free will to the full. Here, beloved, is a very subtle point. You possess free will, but in due time a certain section on your Path starts when you have to sacrifice your free will in order to keep your progress along the Path. Imagine yourself climbing a mountain and having reached a very dangerous section of the Path. There are steep cliffs and abysses ahead. You can keep moving alone as before, but it is more reasonable for you to trust an experienced instructor — a guide who will control your further advancement. And you entrust yourself to the will of this instructor. You have to obey his instructions and recommendations. He watches your progress carefully and tells you where to put your foot and where it is better for you to change the direction of movement in order to reach your goal more quickly— the peak of the Divine consciousness.

Such an instructor, a guide, can be met by you on the physical plane. Yet we must warn you that in the physical plane, it is very difficult for you to meet very pure guides, Teachers, with whom you can fully entrust yourself. Very few people can give you detailed guidance about your Path when you are approaching the peak. Here we have a complete analogy with the instructors who are capable of reaching the highest summit of the world — Chomolungma. Billions of people live on planet Earth now, but only a few are able to climb to the peak Chomolungma.

It is very difficult to distinguish your guides among these billions of people. Many people will tell you that they are true instructors and will offer to take you through training with them for a lot of money. And many of these self-proclaimed teachers will demand that you submit your free will to their will completely.

I repeat once again: In fact, there is a section on the Path where you have to give up your free will partly or completely and to submit your will to the Teacher. A large number of impostors and false teachers take advantage of this truth to get at their disposal light-souls and use their light.

What is the way out? The way out, as always, is in your ability to differentiate, to make distinctions between the Light and the darkness. Generally speaking, the main quality you need on your Path is the quality of making distinctions. You need discipline, you need devotion, aspiration, and constancy, but first you need to make distinctions, because when you step on a dangerous section of the Path and see only bare cliffs ahead and around you, then your life completely depends on the person to whom you entrust your free will.

Therefore, we warn you about this dangerous section of the Path in advance, though for many of you this thorny section is still quite remote in time.

How can you make your distinction? I suppose it is not superfluous to repeat that a true Teacher will never stay in places where crowds of people gather. A true Teacher will never teach for money. A true Teacher will never indulge your pride and your ego. His task is precisely to cut down your arrogance and your ego.

Yet, you can always find a contradiction among the characteristics I have mentioned. You can say, for instance, that Jesus gave his Teaching to the crowds. You can say that Jesus accepted donations and lived on the offerings.

Here lies the difficulty of your stay in the physical world. There are rules, and there are exceptions to these rules. That is why the Path is so difficult, and that is why only a few can take the liberty to follow this Path so far.

We can offer you direct contact with the Ascended Hosts. We are giving these Dictations in order to simplify for you the establishment of this contact. However, you know that the level of your vibrations is determined by the level of your consciousness. But just as like draws to like, you can easily come into interaction with the forces of the astral plane that are not the lightest ones if the level of your vibrations does not allow you to rise to the etheric octaves of Light.

In the end, everything is determined only by you. There is no other being in the Universe that can pass your Path instead of you. You can ask for help, and you may rely on help, but you will go alone and make your choice by yourself. Our task is just to simplify and to secure your Path as best we can. Always remember that your main enemy and source of ill will is hidden inside of you, and this is your carnal mind — your ego.

Everything that enables you to get rid of your ego is beneficial to you. Everything that strengthens and intensifies your ego is not Divine. That is why the disciples who have already reached very high levels of achievement prefer at times to divert from further progress when they approach the section of the Path that demands from them full submission to the will of the Teacher. The thought that the Teacher can hurt the disciple can hardly awaken an echo in the consciousness of the disciple; the Teacher sees your imperfections and sometimes gives you a very painful test to help you get rid of your imperfection.

But your ego perceives this test as an insult or a threat.

If you come to a surgeon and he suggests performing a major operation on you, you can either agree with the upcoming operation or refuse it by your own free will. You can either trust the surgeon's authority or refuse the surgery. You decide it yourself.

But once you lie on the operating table and completely entrust yourself to the surgeon, nothing depends on you any longer. You have made your choice.

The same thing happens when you entrust yourself to a Teacher, and a true Teacher performs a very painful operation to remove your ego. But you go to this operation consciously because you understand that your further progress and your life itself are impossible if you do not get rid of your ego right away.

There is a section of the Path that you will not be able to overcome alone without a guide. As soon as you approach this section, a Teacher will appear. This is reflected in the adage, "When a disciple is ready to learn, a Teacher will appear."

Your task is to make a distinction and not to rush down a slippery road instead of climbing up. What is more, it is not always possible for you to make out the direction of your movement on the Path.

You have been given all the recommendations. You have been warned about all the difficulties. And yet, try to keep your Faith and your Love all along your Path. I also wish the Divine Wisdom always accompanies you on your Path.

I AM Kuthumi.

A Teaching on Buddha and the multiplying of the Buddha consciousness

June 14, 2005

I AM Kuthumi, having come again.

According to the established tradition, I will give a Teaching. However, the comprehension of this Teaching can be difficult for your external consciousness. This is a Teaching on Buddha — on the stage of your Path which you must inevitably reach and which you will reach sooner or later.

Each of you has a potential to become a Buddha. In exactly the same way as every seed has a potential to become a plant and, in turn, to bring forth seeds.

The only thing differentiating you from a Buddha is the level of consciousness.

Some seeds fall on good soil and sprout very quickly. Others require considerable effort for germination. However, you should never forget that all of you are in a garden where the gardener is God. He is a very careful gardener. That is why, even if to become a Buddha requires great efforts from you, you will become a Buddha despite everything. It is impossible for you not to become a Buddha, because this is a natural and obligatory stage of your development. Today I do not want to dwell upon those souls who have no wish to develop and follow the Path that is planned for them. You are aware of the fact that not all the seeds sprout. There are a certain percentage of the seeds that never become mature plants. There are a certain percentage of plants that perish without reaching the stage of the fruiting season.

Yet, you must know what to aim for. And your aim is to become a Buddha.

In fact, the level of the Buddha Consciousness, when you reach it, is akin to a plant entering the fruiting season. When a human reaches the level of the Buddha Consciousness, he obtains an ability to endow with his consciousness millions of beings who are at the lower stages of evolutionary development. This resembles an adult plant scattering seeds.

A Buddha sows the seeds of the Buddha Consciousness within human beings. These seeds lie dormant within a human for some time.

Nevertheless, the time preset by the cosmic terms comes and the seeds of Buddha start to germinate in the human. Buddha sows the sparks of his Mind within the human beings. The time comes and these sparks of Mind germinate and become obvious. Within each of you there is a hidden seed of Buddha, a spark of Mind that was sown in your being millions of years ago according to earthly measures. Now the time is coming when this spark of the Buddha Consciousness begins to be manifested.

This is not the intellect. These are not your abilities enabling you to exist in the physical world. This is the Mind that dwells within you and is identical to the Divine Mind. This is something inside of you that gives you a chance to reach the Divine stage of evolution and become a God-man.

Just as a seed sacrifices itself in order to enable a plant to appear, in exactly the same way Buddha sacrifices himself to give the seeds of Mind an opportunity to germinate within millions of living beings. This is the sublime self-sacrifice that you become capable of when you reach the level of the Buddha Consciousness.

It was the self-sacrifice of the greatest Beings of Light, millions of years ago, that gave humanity a chance to obtain Mind and, thanks to this Mind, to become different from the animals.

You obtained your Mind due to an act of infinite self-sacrifice that was performed by the greatest Beings of Light who blended into the humanity of Earth in the hope that the seeds they planted would germinate and the Buddha Consciousness would multiply someday. And instead of the seven greatest Beings of Light, the Universe would obtain millions of Buddhas.

Thus, development takes place and in this way the merits are multiplied.

However, between the stage when the seeds are sown and the stage when the plant becomes fruit-bearing there is some duration, a natural period. For the humanity of Earth this duration lasts for many millions of years.

The Divine Alchemy is such that the Beings of Light, who sacrificed primordially in order to endow humanity of Earth with Mind, blended into the humans of Earth, in the millions of lifestreams. And they will be able to restore their identity completely only after all the humans, remaining on Earth by that time, have reached the level of the Buddha Consciousness.

Within each of the Ascended Masters there is a spark of a higher Being of Light, and when a person reaches the level of the ascended state of consciousness, he becomes able to give back the spark of Mind that has served as the yeast in the depth of his being and has caused his evolution to take place. The Heavens are exultant over each case of such ascension. Every case of such ascension gives to those Great Spirits, who endowed mankind with the Mind millions of years ago, an opportunity to restore their integrity to a greater extent.

However, when a human reaches the stage of development of a Buddha, he in turn follows the example of the great Beings of Light. Each Ascended Master who has reached the level of Buddha Consciousness has the opportunity to impart a particle of himself to those individuals who are still in embodiment and with whom this Master was karmically connected, and whose life his history of existence on planet Earth was tightly intertwined.

Of course, your lifestream must be in agreement with the presence of a particle of the Ascended Master within you.

I will tell you more. Every prophet, Messenger, or messiah always had the presence of the higher Beings of Light within himself. Sometimes there was not one Being of Light but a few of them. The presence of the Beings of Light within the temple of an embodied individual is determined by his level of merits. You will not be able to endure the Light of the presence of the Higher Being within yourself if you are not ready, if you have not reached a certain level of purity of your four lower bodies, and correspondingly, if you do not have a high level of vibrations corresponding to a high level of consciousness achieved by you.

The knowledge I am giving you today is not new. It was well-known and taught in all the prominent Schools of Mysteries and was echoed in many books and scientific works.

Everything changes, and the time comes when the things that were accessible to very few advanced disciples become attainable for many people. Only the level of your consciousness prevents you from understanding and fully appreciating the greatness of the Creator, His care for every live creature, and the opportunities that the Law of this Universe provides for the evolution of all the souls inhabiting the Universe.

Today I told you a beautiful legend about Buddhas and the multiplying of Buddha Consciousness.

When a seed germinates and the plant grows, it encounters many barriers on its Path of development. These are droughts, floods, the burning sun, and the insect pests. Every individual in his development on planet Earth encounters many barriers. Every individual has to overcome a great many obstacles. However, these obstacles are necessary for the growth of your consciousness. You become a Buddha only when you have overcome all of the obstacles. You become a Buddha only when you go beyond the framework of the illusory world in your consciousness.

Now, here is the most important thing that I must tell you about. The Teaching you have just received is just another view of the fall of Lucifer and the fall of the angels.

As exemplified by these two views on one and the same event, you can judge how unrecognizably the human mind can distort even the highest deed of the Spirit.

In truth, everyone judges everything by himself, and everyone sees in everything his own imperfections.

That is why your own choice about which of the two legends you accept in your external consciousness will tell you a lot about yourself.

The quality of duality is inherent in every event occurring in the material Universe. And the higher the level your consciousness, the less negative and the more positive and Divine things you see in the surrounding reality.

When your consciousness reaches a high enough degree of purity, you will be astonished with the fact that everything around you has changed.

And then, instead of the fallen angels that were surrounding you and with whom you were tirelessly fighting, you will see human beings who suffer and need your help.

In order for the transformation of you and your consciousness to take place, you must wish to move along on the Path, you must put yourself under the winds of change, and not be afraid of anything. Nothing threatens you in your world except your own unreal part that attracts into your world all the negative situations and circumstances.

I wish you to attain enlightenment already during your current life. All the Ascended Hosts and I are ready to serve you and to give you all the help you need.

But never forget: It is impossible to help an individual who does not ask for help and who thinks he does not need our help.

Always remember that you are just children in the questions of knowing the Divine Truth. At the current stage of the development of your consciousness, even the Truth that I have given you today will seem incomprehensible and disquieting to you. But a few years will pass and every school-child will be aware of this Truth.

I AM Kuthumi.

A Teaching on the karma of inactivity

June 24, 2005

I AM Kuthumi, having come again.

Our talk today will be dedicated to the karma of inactivity. Have you ever heard of the karma of inactivity? It seems to you that only your actions can create karma. In the course of our previous talks, you have become familiarized with both the notion of karma[9] and the process of its creation. You have also had a chance to get an insight into good karma[10]. And now I want to return to the topic of karma and to give you a Teaching on the karma of inactivity.

Imagine that someone turns to you for help, but you do not wish to help. Will you create karma in

[9] Refer to the Dictation "A Teaching on karma," Beloved Kuthumi, May 31, 2005 in *Words of Wisdom Volume I*.

[10] Refer to the Dictation "A Teaching on good karma," Beloved Kuthumi, June 6, 2005, in *Words of Wisdom Volume I*.

this case? You will not do anything, will you? You will not make any effort in order to help the person who asks you for help.

Many people on Earth create karma precisely by doing nothing in situations where they should act.

You see that according to the Divine Law you create karma even if you are inactive.

You come into your world in order to act and to gain experience. Consequently, if you avoid acting, you create karma.

Let me give an explanation of this point. You remember that karma is the energy that you qualify incorrectly by performing wrong actions. If the Divine energy coming to you from the Divine world is used by you in accordance with the Divine Law, you create good karma — your treasures in Heaven. If you misuse the Divine energy, then it accumulates in your four lower bodies as negative energy. And in accordance with the Divine Law, this energy attracts to you the situations you have to pass through again and again, in order to learn your lesson, to make a right choice, and thus to work off your karma. For example, if you envy somebody, or take offence at somebody, or you talk behind somebody's back, then you create karma. And this karma will return to you most probably in the form of situations where you yourselves will be treated badly in exactly the same way. You will be envied, or caused offence to, or venomous tongues will talk about you. And in order to work off your karma, you will have to pass through all these situations with humility and obedience to the Will of God, without condemning your offenders, and by being infinitely forgiving to the people who harm you.

That is why Jesus said that you should forgive "seventy times seven."[11] You never know how many times in your past lives you offended people and allowed yourselves to behave abominably towards them.

And now let us return to the karma of inactivity.

Imagine that a man asks for your help, and you refuse to help him. Will you create karma by acting in this way? You do not waste the Divine energy, do you? You just do not do anything. This situation is not as simple as it may seem. And whether you will or will not create karma in this case depends on many conditions.

First of all, you must be sure that a person who turns to you for help really needs it. If a person asks for your help and does not need it but you give him this help anyway, then this person creates karma. You do not create karma in this case, but indirectly you help the other person to create karma. When you reach a certain spiritual level, you are obliged

---

[11] Matthew 18:22

not only to attend to your affairs but also to help other people avoid situations in which they create karma.

And now comes the next moment. If a person who turns to you for help really needs it, you will not create karma if you refuse this person because you cannot help him.

It may be that a person is in a difficult situation and is really in urgent need of help, such as financial assistance. And he turns to you for help. But if you have no opportunity to help this person or you think you should primarily use your money to feed your family, you do not create karma in this case. It is highly probable that the person who turns to you for help refused to help you in a past life when you asked him, and now you are simply returning his karmic debt to him.

And finally, if a person turns to you for help and really needs help, but you refuse to help him although you can do it, then you create karma.

You are obliged to help the people who ask you for help. When you can help but refuse to, it seems to you that you are not wasting Divine energy and, consequently, are not creating karma. However, the feelings and motives that guide you toward this decision cause you to create karma. For example, you want to teach this person a lesson, or it is pleasant for you when someone is humiliated before you, or you are too lazy to help somebody, or you are driven by greed. Any of these qualities and many other such character traits, when they are the true reason for your refusal to help, are non-divine qualities and you create karma by manifesting them.

Therefore, before you refuse to help a person who asks you for help, always carefully weigh all pros and cons.

Your best adviser in a difficult situation is undoubtedly your Higher Self, because your Higher Self always knows whether you should give help or not. If your connection with your Higher Self is impeded or you are not sure about the answers received, then carefully analyze your inner motive and feelings. Maybe you do not want to help this person because you either cannot be bothered, or you pinch pennies, or grudge the time, or you start condemning this person for having deteriorated to such a state that he cannot solve his problems himself. If such thoughts come into your head, try to overcome these thoughts and force yourself to render the help you are asked for. And after you have given help, you will feel a relief and this will be a sign that you have done the right thing and worked out some old karma of the past.

If you do not feel any negative feelings, but your intuition suggests that you should not help a person in spite of the fact that the person needs help, asks you for it, and you are able to help him, that means there could be a one percent chance that you are giving the person who turns to you a test. And you refuse him precisely because of the fact that you are fiving this person a test. However, tests like this are very rare, and you must possess a high spiritual level and go through initiations to be granted the mantle of a Guru in order to have a right to give such tests. Therefore, I recommend that you always help a person who needs help and asks you for help when you are able to do so.

In reality, many problems in your world are due precisely to the fact that people ask for help and do not receive it — for example, from officials who are supposed to give help and even receive salary appendant to their position for this purpose, but who do not give the help to the people asking them.

You should always remember that in your next life you will reverse roles, and the official who does not perform his duty properly due to his neglect will find himself in a pleading position and will have to appeal for help exactly to those individuals whom he refused to help.

Exactly the same problem arises for the high and mighty that are very wealthy. Great wealth is always evidence that this person's karma is connected with a wrong attitude toward money.

Wealth is given to people as a chance to work off such karma. Therefore, a person on whom wealth drops from the clouds to enable him to work off his karma should very carefully analyze how he can dispose of this wealth to help to as many needy people as possible. Yet, he should specifically give help to the destitute and not waste money on theatrical philanthropy. For if a person wrongly disposes of his wealth and wastes it on pleasures or objects of luxury and prestige, it is 99 percent probable that in his next life he will receive the return of his karma and will be born into a very poor family, and he will be begging door-to door all his life barely making ends meet.

Thus, never envy those people who possess great wealth. Great wealth is evidence of great karma in the present and, if used wrongly, then of a greater karma in the future.

I think our talk has been effective today. At the very least, this knowledge can help you avoid the karma of inactivity in your lives.

I AM Kuthumi.

Are you ready to enter the Path?

June 29, 2005

I AM Kuthumi, having come to you today.

A matter of great concern for us, the Ascended Hosts, is the rise of the consciousness of humanity, and we devote rapt attention to this task and exert every effort for its accomplishment. If we managed to shift the entire mass of human consciousness at least a millimeter, then the changes in the world around you would not be long in manifesting themselves.

In reality, there is nothing in the material world that is as difficult to change as human consciousness, because everything else is subject to the change of consciousness and happens very quickly and almost automatically.

Therefore, our mission, as well as your main task, is to change the consciousness of people who are embodied now.

I will give you a simple example. When you do some work, you should first make a plan of this work in your mind or get an idea of it in your consciousness in order to clarify what exactly you want to achieve in the course of your work and what should be the result of your actions. The same can be said about the change of consciousness of mankind. The majority of mankind should realize the need to change their consciousness and understand what steps they should take in this direction. The subsequent actions will be just a matter of technique. The materialization of the conceived idea will take place automatically and inevitably as soon as the image to which the people should aspire is firmly settled in their consciousness. That is why the forces that multiply the illusion of the physical world have learned very well to take advantage of the latest scientific and technical achievements in order to maintain in the consciousness of people the wrong stereotypes of behavior and the incorrect standards that people follow in their lives.

The whole power of the mighty industry of the contemporary world is aimed at multiplying the illusion. The best human minds exert their efforts with only one purpose — to make people direct their attention to the things that multiply the illusion. But you know that your energy flows where your attention is directed. Thus, when unavoidably looking through advertising video clips, advertising literature or posters, you automatically involve your energies in the multiplication of the illusion of your world. The sophistication of the industry that uses your Divine energy for the multiplication of the illusion knows no bounds. People care only about the acquisition of objects and goods that are imposed upon their consciousness from the outside. The desire to possess nice trivialities is kindled. And a person has to waste more and more efforts and energy chasing after new things. He starts lacking the energy given to him by God, and in order to continue this chase, he stirs himself up with drugs and tranquillizers. And right up to their forties, the majority of humans feel so drained inside by this endless thirst for pleasures and goods that they are simply unable to take into their consciousness the things that are told in these Dictations.

Moreover, the age at which people come to such inner lethargy is decreasing with every year. A lot of young people get involved in the endless rush for the pleasures and objects of this world even from childhood. This cycle goes on from life to life. And now the tension from the process of forcing the thirst for pleasures and goods has reached such a high point of intensity of emotions that hardly anybody can stand this frenzied race for pleasures and delights.

Only when a person drops out of this chase due to some debilitating disease and finds himself back at the bottom of the ladder does he begin finally to think about the simplest things that he should have thought about in the dawn of his life. Why has he come to this world? What is the meaning of his existence in the material world? That is why it is advisable that you should not bring your life to a complete collapse before you start thinking about such vital things as the meaning of your existence in the material world. Do not bring your life to a shipwreck. Find the strength within yourself to stop, to step aside from this frantic race for pleasures, goods, and delights. And try to observe from the side those people who waste their invaluable lives and the energy granted to them by God to multiply the illusion, because all their thoughts and aspirations are completely focused on the illusory world.

Your task is to trace all the moments of your life when you waste your Divine energy, not for the Divine purposes but for the purposes of this world. There is nobody outside you who can force you to pursue the pleasures from some extra trinket, or a modern concert, from a football match, or from resting at a prestigious resort. It is only you who make yourselves chase after all these unnecessary things. Your lusts, your carnal mind, and all that is unreal in you make you do so. That is why this Teaching is being given to you — a Teaching on the rejection of the unreal part of yourself. Remember history, remember the prophets who were stoned and crucified on the cross. Why did this happen? It happened because the carnal mind, spurred with the desire for the continuation of the pleasures of the physical world, was ready to kill everyone who preached the Path of refusal from the illusory world.

In fact, all the people embodied now are possessed by their carnal minds. In order for a person to realize all the absurdity of his situation, God puts him into such situations that can give him the most important lessons. And every time a person gets into a situation from which he should draw a moral lesson, this situation becomes more and more intense until it reaches the point of absurdity, and only a deaf or a blind man could not understand the lesson that life gives him. Each of you encounters such situations in the course of your life. And each of you is provided with repeated opportunities to make the one and only right choice. But every time, you prefer to give up making this choice and continue serving the objects of this world and are bound to the chariot of your carnal mind.

God is patient. God is exceptionally patient. Sometimes a person might spend his whole life or even several lives in order to recognize one single quality that he should get rid of.

You have some time ahead of you to discern all your imperfections and get rid of them. But the main thing for you is to make your choice and to start your progress on the Path of giving up your ego, on the Path of your return to the real world of God.

This very first and most important step in the right direction can become so decisive for you that it will change your whole life in a few years. You can waste millions of years more, wandering around the illusory world. But when you take one step in the right direction and then continue to progress, however difficult it may be and whatever trials you have to get through on your Path, you make the right choice, and this choice will become the key to your victory and your exodus from the world of the illusion into the Divine world.

This world exists only within your consciousness, and you maintain the existence of this world with your consciousness. For that reason, you must transit onto a new level of your consciousness and understanding of the reality around you in order to leave the physical world and to obtain Divine freedom. There is nobody, no one person who can force you to make your choice. You and only you can make this far-reaching decision alone in the quiet of your heart.

Never forget that you will receive no reward in the physical world and that you should never think about getting any benefits for yourself in the physical world. All your achievements and experience will remain with you during the entire period of existence of this Universe and will transit together with you to the Higher Worlds.

Are you ready to enter the Path and to follow it tirelessly towards your victory through all the barriers and difficulties?

Many are called, but how many are chosen?

I AM Kuthumi, with a hope for you in my heart.

A Teaching on Karma descending at the end of the year

December 19, 2005

I AM Kuthumi. I have come to you through our Messenger.

I have come to give you a Teaching on how you should regard the karma that descends upon you at the end of the year. What is this karma, and how you should treat its descending?

You know that your four lower bodies contain energetic records about wrong, dishonest, and non-divine acts that you committed during your present or one of your past lives. These can be records of persistent negative states that you were experiencing in the past and have not been able to get rid of up to this day.

You are aware that karma returns to you. You are aware of the karma that is activated within your aura in accordance with the Law of Cosmic Cycles and arises in front of you in the form of some situation, feeling, or poor state of your consciousness. This return of karma happens continuously and gradually during the year. But when the annual cycle is nearly over, you come up against a slightly different situation. It might happen that the karma, which has been returning to you during the year in accordance with the Cosmic Law, has not been worked off by you as much as required by the Law. Imagine that during this particular one-year cycle other people have also not been able to work off their karma by making right choices, praying, or committing good deeds.

In this case, at the end of the year there is an accumulation of surplus karma that looms over humanity and is ready to descend in the form of various states inherent to humankind (diseases, depression, hunger), or in the form of various cataclysms and natural disasters.

In any case, at the end of the year, even with your inner sensation you can feel that you are experiencing some increased heaviness. This is just the extra karmic burden that lies on humanity in the form of non-transmuted negative energy.

That is why it is so important to maintain increased discipline of your consciousness at the end of the year. It is very helpful for you to consciously impose limitations upon yourselves (such as fasting, practicing silence, prayer vigils, or helping the poor and underprivileged) that you can bring as a sacrifice to the altar of Service.

In this case, you create additional good karma that in the most extreme circumstances can be used for the purpose of balancing the situation on the planet.

That is why we come to you during this new cycle of Dictations and remind you again and again about the possibility of a cataclysm or a natural disaster. Not because we want to scare you and make you pray. No, we come to explain to you the current difficult situation on Earth and offer those of you who are ready to act as co-creators with God and the Hierarchy of Light existing in the Universe.

If your consciousness is not ready for such service, then it is likely that you will perceive our requests as unreasonable intimidation.

However, let's reason upon this together. What is the alternative? How else can the excessive masses of negative energy accumulated on the planet be eliminated? Do you think a miracle will happen and all the energy that you have not been able to work off in the given one-year period will just miraculously vanish?

All such miracles, even if they happened in the past, always required a great amount of additional energy. This energy was granted to your planet either from the cosmic reserves or from the causal bodies of the Ascended Masters.

Now imagine a company that shows unprofitable results year after year. The owner of the company borrows funds from other companies — profitable ones — and covers the loss. This can last for some period of time. But there comes a time when the owner realizes that the loss is not a random occurrence but is due to the negligence of the employees of this company.

So, a good owner can either make his employees work better or close the company.

The measures being taken now by the Ascended Hosts are aimed at encouraging the best representatives of mankind to work better. You do not want to lose your workplace — your planet if using the above analogy — do you?

Therefore, it is necessary to have a clear understanding of the alternative the planet is facing at the present moment. You will either be able to take responsibility for the situation on the planet, or you will be deprived of the opportunity to continue the evolution on this planet because it will be recognized as a dead-end.

Of course, all this will not happen right away. You will be given the opportunity to gradually realize your responsibility. In order to make our persuasions more convincing, you were warned earlier[12] that we would no longer restrain the karma that is being created by people living in particular locations. And this karma will almost immediately return in the form of some kind of man-made or natural disaster. The probability of such cataclysms increases by the end of the year. That is why you are strongly recommended to approach your spiritual practices, prayers, and meditations more consciously at the end of the year.

There are people whose consciousness is at such a low level that it is useless to speak to them about such things. But luckily for them, their extent of karmic responsibility is low in comparison with those individuals who realize all the complexity of the situation, but due to their inherent imperfections, laziness, and shortsightedness they do not take those actions that we ask them for.

Depending on the level of consciousness reached by people, the Law of Karma operates in different ways. And what can be forgiven for some people is unforgivable for others. You should not care about the fact that somebody's behavior is

---

[12] Refer to the Dictation "Each of your acts of service to all the living creatures reduces the probability of the next threatening cataclysm," Lord of the World Gautama Buddha, May 2, 2005, in *Words of Wisdom Volume 1*.

improper but still no karma descends upon them to teach them a lesson.

Purely and simply, this person has either enough time for his evolution or a sufficient supply of good karma. Do not worry. The Karmic Law operates impeccably. And everyone will receive an opportunity to encounter the karma that they created in the past.

Do not think about others, think about yourself. Think about how you personally can mitigate your karma, your family's karma, and the karma of your country and planet.

You may not understand all the details of how this universal Law operates, but you should have a general idea about this Law, and you should tell those who are not yet familiar with the Law of Karma about it. The more people who know about this Universal Law, the greater is the probability that they will avoid committing improper deeds in their lives.

When karma descends upon you, most commonly you are unable to observe the cause and effect relationship between the actions you committed and their consequences that descend upon you in the form of different misfortunes and illnesses. And you exclaim, "Why, Lord?" instead of accepting with humility everything that God sends you.

Believe me, God is very merciful. The karma that descends upon you returns to you in the easiest possible way. If you had an opportunity to understand which of your actions burden you with some type of karmic responsibility, then you would thank God for allowing you to so mercifully work off what you deserve because of what you yourselves committed in the past.

There are several ways of working off your karma.

The first way is not to create karma at all.

The second way is to work off your karma by making right choices.

The third way is to work off your karma by accepting with humility any situation that you get into.

Finally, you can mitigate your karmic burden by prayer and true repentance. This is what we suggest you should do intensely during the time remaining until the end of this year. Now you have an opportunity to realize that everything that the Masters ask of you is justified and reasonable. None of us has an intention to scare you and force you do something.

We speak to you as sensible people who are standing just slightly lower on the steps of the evolutionary ladder.

I AM Kuthumi, and I was happy to share a seed of my knowledge with you.

Only when you receive the Law from within your heart, do you become the executor of the Law

April 28, 2006

I AM Kuthumi, having come to you again.

It has been several months since our previous meeting, and today I am extremely happy about our new meeting, because this meeting will take place in much more favorable conditions, and I will be able to give you the Teaching that was impossible to give earlier. This is the Teaching on how you should perceive life and on how you should perceive the changes that are occurring in your life. Some time ago, this Teaching would be irrelevant for you. But now more and more people are thinking about their life surroundings and about their attitudes to all that. This new view of life and the conditions around you has become possible after the Teaching about the contraction of illusion that was given through our Messenger. Therefore, you have subconsciously started to relate differently to everything around you, and you began to think about creating circumstances around you and about your influence on everything around you in the physical world.

This is the new view of the world. The bigger the number of people who realize that the world around represents a gigantic illusion and that the manifestation of this illusion is completely determined by the collective consciousness of mankind, the more conscious your attitude to your thoughts, feelings, and actions will be; for it is you who create everything around you and all the circumstances of your life. The fact that the changes that have occurred in your consciousness take their time to be manifested in the physical world is just determined by the inertness of matter and by the impossibility for it to appear instantly in front of you in its new form. Another hindering function is that the consciousness of the majority of mankind has not yet awakened and cannot have such critical influence as the consciousness of those people who have started to realize the Divine Laws and try to follow them in their lives.

Therefore, it is in your interests and in the interests of all of mankind to spread these Teachings and this Knowledge that you receive through our Messages as widely as possible. You can notice that the information that you receive does not differ much from the fundamentals of most of religions of the world. Still, there is a slight difference and the difference is due to the fact that we direct you to an individual inner Path, the Path of knowing the world through your hearts. Any external knowledge comes to you from outside you, and therefore, you are inclined not to trust that knowledge. When you become capable of receiving the information coming from within you, then you take that information in a completely different way. Even if it does not contain anything new for you, all the incoming knowledge is interpreted in a different way and it comes home to your consciousness.

There are different stages of perception of information. When you realize in your outer mind that you already know this and have heard it before, it does not mean that you have deeply felt this information and this Teaching in your heart and have realized it to the extent that you become one with this Knowledge and Teaching. Only when you become one with the Teaching, do you become a bearer of this Teaching, and you inseparably link your life with it and submit to the Law that you have accepted with your whole being.

There are different stages of awareness of the Divine Law, and only when you receive this Law from the depths of your heart, do you become the executor of the Law, and you are able to influence the life around you without words and without actions. You acquire an ability to influence the environment around you by your presence. You just meditate, stay in a state of bliss and contentment, and the life around you changes as if by magic.

That is a very high level of achievement to which all of you should aspire. But in order for you to have a state of deep meditation in your world, you should think about creating the conditions for such meditations. Your cities and even less populated places are filled with so much negative energy that it is difficult for you to get in touch with your Higher Self, as well as being hard for us to reach your consciousness, which is constantly shielded by negative energies. Therefore, again and again we draw your attention to the conditions in which you live. You should have a chance to stay alone and apply efforts to spend some time in places where you can restore your energy. Then, when you gain the standard of the Divine state within yourselves, you will know where to aspire, and you will limit the influence of the negative energies that abound in your world around you. We give you a chance to compare your vibrations with the vibrations of our incarnated representative on Earth so that you do not lose your Path. We drop a lifeline to you, and your decision whether to accept our help or not.

At all times there were incarnated people who were carrying Divine vibrations of purity. And there are such people among you. If your eyes were open and your ears could hear, then every day you would thank God for sending His incarnated Messengers to you. But you go past them without taking notice.

Therefore, it is your first duty to note the manifestation of Divinity in the people around you and to help such people, because they carry the burden of your karma.

In the East, the veneration of saints and yogis is very common; they incarnate specifically to take people's karma upon themselves in order to transmute it. In the West, there are also many people incarnated who are not of this world and who take and carry the burden of your karma. Learn to be grateful to such people. They cannot always adapt to the conditions of your society, because for these people your society is like a society of crazy people. However, you hurry to announce that your saints are insane. Your world is upside-down. The least worthy have everything while those who bear the burden of mankind eke out a miserable existence. However, it has always been this way throughout modern history.

Your world is an upside-down world. And when you learn to recognize the manifestation of Divinity in your world and in your consciousness separate it from any non-divine manifestation, then you will really be able to influence the world around you and transform it.

But first you should learn to recognize the Divine manifestation within yourself. Then you will be able to draw similar Divine manifestations from space according to your vibrations. The islets of Divinity will expand and multiply in your world, and we will be able to come to you, first in our denser bodies and then in our more subtle bodies. And the prophecy about the Ascended Masters walking among you will come true, and you will be able to communicate with us.

Therefore, it depends only on you to make the prophecy a reality in your time.

Create the islets of Divinity and move to them, at least for a while.

I AM Kuthumi.

Expanding the understanding of the Law of Karma

July 6, 2006

I AM Kuthumi, who has come to you today.

During the period of time when we did not meet with you, I had the opportunity to analyze and comprehend the responsibility that our communication puts on you and on me. If you think about it, then you will come to the inevitable conclusion that everything that happens during our communication with you through the Dictations has an astonishing value and must be treated with respect and care. At first you may not realize this and attach little significance to our Messages, but as you read our Messages and dive into our energies, you appreciate more and more the minutes of our communication and assess the quality of our Messages and the possibility of communicating with us and. So, I have come today to speak with you as with old friends. Moreover, I can tell you that I meet many of you almost daily during your night's sleep in my retreat on the etheric plane.

When the knowledge that you receive from me in the course of our communication in the retreat finds an external confirmation in these Dictations, it germinates within your consciousness, and you begin to do many things consciously in the physical plane. Your consciousness begins to comprehend the truths that could not otherwise penetrate your dense world.

So we continue our mutual work to transform your physical world. This work of ours does not presuppose your blind obedience to our advice and recommendations, but it implies a creative application of all the knowledge you have received in your lives. We do not need blind followers who are ready to do what we tell them to do at our first call. We need conscientious, serious-minded disciples who do not just mindlessly do something, but consciously reflect the received knowledge in their external consciousness and find the best scenario to optimally implement our plans.

Thus, you join in with the cosmic co-creation. We highly value those of our disciples who do not run from one teacher to another in search of advice on how to behave in daily life situations, but who are able to raise their consciousness above the day-to-day chores and see the prospects that open up and set them in motion without waiting for ideal conditions to develop on the physical plane. You are able to evolve only by overcoming yourselves and the hardships that surround you in your lives. You should not be afraid of life's problems and the failures that await you. The whole point is your attitudes to these problems and failures. The Teaching provides you with correct approaches. You yourselves, guided by these approaches, create your lives.

You change your consciousness and begin to see the problems that you face in life differently. You analyze the problems and obstacles that confront you, and you thank God that He has given you the opportunity to understand your past mistakes and to correct them through your right attitude to the arising problems.

You should never give in to disappointment and depression. You receive the Teaching in order to form within yourselves proper attitudes to the things you come across and that accompany you in your lives. If some of you, with my help or based on your inner intuition (a hint from your Higher Self), suddenly understand the reason why a certain karmic situation was brought into your life, then you will start giving countless thanks to God for allowing you to work off your karmic debt in such an easy way.

Truly is the grace of Heaven endless, and only by your irrational behavior were you able to generate the reasons for the problems and disasters that you face in life. Sometimes these problems are so big that your whole life literally crosses off your chance to render your service to the Brotherhood fully. That is because you are too burdened with your karmic debts. Yet, the wisdom you gain through our communication helps you to understand that in your future life that you will be able to continue your service, and you will receive such circumstances in your lives that will not be so difficult and burdensome. That is because during your present life you have already worked off most of your karmic debts. Because you have worked off these debts yourselves, your children will carry a much lighter burden as well. It is because the property of karma is such that sometimes the karmic load that has not been worked off comes down as a heavy burden on children and grandchildren. Therefore, be glad about the misfortunes and miseries that come down on you. Thus, you prepare a bright future for yourselves in your next life and for your children and grandchildren in their present lives. The proper understanding of the Law of Karma makes you happy even when you carry an intolerable karmic load from the point of view of the people around you.

The whole point is in the attitude of your external consciousness to the burden that you are carrying. Therefore, never be saddened by your problems. Allow yourselves to be happy with the fact that by overcoming your current problems you are preparing a bright future for yourselves and your children and grandchildren.

The next generation will be much happier than you, because many of you have taken on karmic responsibilities that are too big to work off during this life. You did this deliberately to accelerate the process of changes on planet Earth. The people around you, who point at you and say that you have probably committed too much sin because your burden is so heavy, understand nothing about the operation of the Law of Karma, and their consciousness is unable to grasp the size of the sacrifice you have taken upon yourselves voluntarily before your incarnation. However, we, the Ascended Hosts, highly value your sacrifice. Moreover, we are ready to respond to your requests and help you as much as the Law allows in order to ease your burden. Sometimes, when the good karma (created by you during your current incarnation) allows, we are able to answer your call and help you in a situation where it seems that you do not have the strength to endure it any longer. Then, a while after your call, you look back with surprise and realize that an insurmountable burden that lay on your shoulders has suddenly disappeared, vanished, fallen off your shoulders. In such a case, never forget to glorify the Heavens and send your gratitude. The best gratitude for us will be the service that you can render for the benefit of life on Earth.

Now I will give you a formula that will enable you to get relief from your karmic burden if your good karma allows you to. So, you say:

"In the name of I AM THAT I AM, in the name of my mighty I AM Presence, in the name of my holy Christ Self (or simply in the name of Almighty God), I appeal to the Great Karmic Board and ask you to use the momentum of my righteous achievements for the purpose of neutralizing the karma which has led to... (you should describe the situation for which you wish to receive help from the Karmic Board).

May all things take place in accordance with the Will of God."

You can write a letter addressed to the Karmic Board, read your call aloud, and burn the letter. If the amount of your accumulated good karma allows, and the Karmic Board decides that your request can be granted, then your karmic situation will be resolved to a greater or lesser extent.

In accordance with the opportunity given to you earlier,[13] you will be called in your subtle body during your night's sleep to a Karmic Board session

---

[13] Refer to the Dictation, "Let your consciousness go beyond the limits of your family, your city, and your country and take the whole Earth as your native home," Lord Maitreya, June 5, 2006, *Words of Wisdom Volume 2.*

and your soul will have to confirm your request, which you had written in your outer consciousness.

Sometimes there are cases when a person's external consciousness does not want to endure the karmic load any longer, but the soul of that person refuses the help. In that case, the Karmic Board listens to the opinion of your soul. Therefore, if your request is not granted after some time, you can talk to your soul and try to come to an agreement with it on this question.

I highly recommend that you practice talking to your soul and write letters to the Karmic Board only after you and your soul have reached an agreement.

You are multilayered beings. You have many bodies. That is why you need to achieve harmony and unity among all your bodies. The bodies of most people are unbalanced to such an extent that they cannot even understand how they should act in the best interest of all the bodies. Stop associating yourselves with just what you see in the mirror. You are much more than your physical body. The next stage in the evolution of mankind will be the understanding of your Higher nature and the creation of harmonious conditions for your Higher nature to manifest itself. That is because the conditions that you are living in now sometimes do not encourage you to bring your subtle bodies into harmony. This is the next stage in the development of mankind. However, right now you should be concerned about creating an environment for the harmonious development of all your bodies.

I have given you a lot of new information today. And I am leaving you with a hope of new meetings.

I AM Kuthumi.

You must constantly analyze the consequences of your actions and try not to teach where your teaching will be immediately dragged through the mire

December 26, 2006

I AM Kuthumi, having come to you today through our Messenger. I have come to give you yet another piece of our Teaching that you have to assimilate, because the time for it has come. The present time is such that every manifestation of the Divinity you meet in life becomes a feast-day for your souls because your souls have been yearning for the Divine world where they came from and where it is time to return now. That is why I am always happy to convey a Message from the Divine world to you and to give you short instructions.

I know that many of you love me and talk to me. And when you are attuned to my wavelength,

I can hear you and perceive your thoughts because this is the way that I serve. So, I know about many of you. And I am aware of the problems that you are burdened with. Therefore, I would like to do everything possible and everything in my power to show you the roots of the problems facing you and give you the impetus necessary to overcome within you the causes of your difficulties.

So, today we will talk about what is relevant and important for many of you. And this is connected to your relationships with the people around you who do not understand and accept your teaching, your guidance, your way of life, and your world-view. Unfortunately, all people are at completely different stages of development. And by the level of your consciousness, many of you still belong to the previous Fourth Root Race. The majority of you belong to different sub-races of the Fifth Root Race, and there is a certain number — a very small number — of individuals who belong to the final sub-races of the Fifth Root Race, and an even smaller number of individuals belonging to the Sixth Root Race, whose time has not yet come, but whose first pioneers, the especially impatient ones, have undertaken their trial embodiments now.

The history of the development of the races is a matter for a time-consuming discussion and will not be the subject of this Dictation. All I want is to direct your attention to an indisputable fact that all of you are standing at different stages of your evolutionary development. And that is why the differences in your consciousness are sometimes so great, and the spheres of your interests and the levels of your consciousness differ so much that sometimes it seems that you speak different languages. Therefore, when you once again have a desire to start teaching or propagate your views among those who you think need a sermon, remember this Dictation and call to mind the words of Jesus, "Do not cast your pearls before swine."[14]

All that is given must be given according to the level of consciousness. And many things that seem to be so obvious to you that you have already stopped paying attention to them can shock the people who do not share your views. Even worse, it can create in them a whole range of negative emotions and even actions. And who do you think will bear the karma of these negative manifestations? If you have not guessed yet, I will prompt you: the karma will fall on you. This is because a human standing at a higher stage of evolutionary development takes full karmic responsibility not only for his or her actions but also for the actions of the people whom he or she provoked into wrong actions.

---

[14] Do not give dogs what is holy, and do not throw your pearls before pigs, lest they trample them underfoot and turn to attack you. (Matthew 7:6).

This does not mean that people whom you provoke are completely freed from karma for their wrong actions. I only want to say that most of the karma will fall on you, because you provoked them into performing the wrong actions. Therefore, before you start preaching and giving anyone advice about how to act in life, think repeatedly about whether you should do it.

Your responsibility is directly proportional to the stage of the evolutionary ladder you occupy.

This does not mean that you should close yourself off and stop communicating with people and talking to them about spiritual topics. Simply, you must constantly analyze the consequences of your actions and try not to teach where your teaching will be immediately dragged through the mire.

Think about my words. And always remember that the best example will be your own behavior in life and the way you react to any life situations and disturbances. All of your preaching will be in your actions. And by the fruits of your actions, people will recognize in you a person who is worth heeding and whose advice is worth seeking. Again I am driving at the fact that the only person in this world with whom you should seriously concern yourself with is you. And you are the most worthy recipient of all your strengths and abilities.

Do not think that somebody acts imperfectly, and do not think about how he should act. Focus on yourself and think about why the actions and words of other people irritate you. Isn't it because everything that irritates you is present within you as a manifestation of your past wrong actions?

The physical world around you is a mirror reflecting your imperfect consciousness. Therefore, it would be natural to assume that if someone regularly meets with ignorance and misunderstanding, then these qualities are present in him or her. And if you are constantly exposed to malicious attacks from other people, then it means that it is the negative energy in you that makes people act that way toward you.

We have covered today's material many times. And you have certainly heard and read about this many times. However, your thoughts, your own thoughts that you send me, make me repeat this small Teaching and remind you about those Truths that you know well but for some reason do not risk applying to yourselves.

I am happy with the opportunity to repeat this Teaching for you. And I will be even happier if some of you can apply this Teaching in practice. And even if it seems to you that everything I have told you has nothing to do with you, do not rush to put this Dictation away and to shelve it. Try to reread this

Message at least three times on different days, at different times of the day, and when you are in different states of consciousness. And I think that by the third time you read it, you will start to understand that this Dictation is directly relevant to you personally.

Trust me, I know human psychology very well, and at times it gives me pleasure to solve the puzzles made up of those psychological problems that you yourselves have created during thousands and thousands of embodiments on Earth. However, I am always glad to help you. And I always answer the requests that you sincerely pronounce in your hearts while looking at my picture or that you risk writing on paper and sending to me by the perfect mail where our angels work. Do you know that when you burn a letter and make a call for the angels of protection to deliver the letter to me or to any other Ascended Master, the physical letter burns but its energetic higher substance is immediately delivered to the address you specified?

I have been happy to give you a small Teaching today.

I AM Kuthumi, with great Love toward you and with a desire to help.

A Teaching about your soul

January 6, 2007

I AM Kuthumi, having come to you again.

As always, I have come to give you the instructions that you need and that your soul needs, yearning for the real Divine world.

We come time after time to take care of your soul and give it the nourishment that it needs. And today I have come to give you a small Teaching about your soul and for your soul.

Let us think together for a minute about what your soul is. Does your soul represent your entire manifested self?

What is meant by soul?

Actually, you are a very complex entity. You have your Divine part located in the Divine world that has never left the Divine world. You also have a soul, the part of you that has been specially created by the builders of form for your journey through the manifested worlds. And your physical body represents a vessel for your soul for the period of earthly incarnations.

You have a very complicated structure. If it were not for the call of the time, I would not come to give you this important Teaching about your soul.

The point is that many of you are confused by what the term soul means.

Your soul is closely and inseparably connected to your physical body, but the connection of your soul with your more subtle Divine bodies was lost at some point during the development of your soul. This was caused by the turning point when you wished to leave the Divine world and to descend into matter. You wished to acquire human experience; it was necessary for the evolution of your soul because your soul could not evolve without the experience of human evolution. It is impossible to develop if you do not constantly gain deeper experience. You descend into a more and more dense manifestation of the physical world, and it looks like your soul and your Higher Self descend to the bottom of the physical ocean in a bathyscaphe. In this case, your physical body serves as a bathyscaphe, and your soul inseparably connected with it, represents your subtle bodies: your astral body, your mental body, and your etheric body. Your subtle bodies are inseparably connected with your physical body and evolve thanks to your physical body.

If we return to the analogy with a bathyscaphe, then your subtle bodies represent the electronic systems and life support systems of your bathyscaphe.

But the bathyscaphe can perform certain tasks at the bottom of the ocean only if it is operated by a person.

Many of you are in such a state of consciousness when the control of the bathyscaphe is lost. Your subtle Divine bodies lose the connection with the bathyscaphe, and the bathyscaphe moves on its own.

Another example that can be used is the image of a sailboat that has lost control in a storm. You live your merely physical life and do not think about who you are, where you came from, and where you are going. This restricts your goals and tasks to the physical world only and prevents you from further development.

There was a stage when you needed to gain the experience of descending into matter, the experience of your embodiments. Your subtle bodies and your soul have managed to evolve and to become more perfect during your journey through matter. Your structure became more and more sophisticated. But at a certain point, you lost the oneness with your soul. You ceased to perceive the Higher worlds and lost the connection with your soul. Your soul became separated from you as well as your subtle bodies. This caused your soul to suffer. You lost many parts of your soul during your numerous incarnations. Your soul suffered very much when you allowed inharmonious behavior and explicit ungodly actions, and those sufferings made your soul partially leave you. That is why your subtle bodies bear imperfections of your previous embodiments from your very birth.

You must understand that there is a more subtle part of you. This is your soul, which is like a little child. Many manifestations of your world hurt your soul badly. It shrinks and can even leave your physical body. But without your soul you lose the ability to manifest Divine feelings. You lose the connection with the Divine world even more, because it is through your soul that your Higher Self can manifest itself.

You need to return to the harmonious development of your soul, your physical body, and your Higher Self. All your bodies need to be balanced and harmonized.

You need to gather all the lost fragments of your soul in order to be able to move to the next step of your evolution. You need to restore your integrity, inner harmony, and peace.

This can be achieved by special practices and methods. Each period of time revealed new practices and new methods that could adjust your subtle bodies. Each method was appropriate for that particular time.

Now, as new energies and vibrations have come to Earth, the best thing for your soul is to spend time in the quiet of nature. There are still corners on the globe where nature has not been exposed to the devastating influence of civilization. These places must serve as refuges and clinics for you. Staying there, you will be able to restore the integrity of your soul, your body, and your Divine part.

You will not be able to achieve this in big cities.

You will need some time to restore your energies.

If you manage to practice your meditations in nature for as much as possible, then gradually you will be able to attract all the fragments of your soul from space. Then, as soon as your soul feels your love and care, it will be attracted to you from space and will never leave you on your path.

I am trying to give you a very important Teaching. I am trying to bring home to your consciousness the fact that your further evolution is impossible unless you manage to restore the integrity of your soul and the harmony between all your bodies.

In nature, it will happen naturally. Then, as soon as you manage to heal your soul and cure its centuries-old wounds, you will be able to serve as an example for those people who are tired of living in the hell of your technocratic civilization. In a natural way your civilization will be able to return to the path that was originally planned for it: the path of spiritual evolution and development of Divine abilities and opportunities.

No matter how you try to assure yourself that you have integrity and you are harmonious, I must tell you that the harmony you achieve with the help of self-hypnosis has nothing to do with the natural harmony, which all of you will certainly attain.

I have given you an important Teaching, a Teaching about your soul.

I AM Kuthumi.

Guidance for every day

June 26, 2007

I AM Kuthumi, who has come to you on this day.

The purpose of my visit today is to give you certain understanding of the future plans of the Brotherhood for the current moment.

Again and again we come, clarify, and give the understanding of many things that are known to you already. Yet, the facets that open up for you allow you to enjoy the new brilliance of the precious stones of the good old knowledge.

We come and you become filled with our energy and our Love again. That is because it is impossible to give the Teaching and not to Love at the same time. All knowledge and understanding come with the feeling of deep, unconditional Love. We give our knowledge based on Love, and you are able to comprehend the information that we provide only when you are able to feel deep unconditional Love for me, for other Masters, and for our Messenger.

Only based on the feelings of Divine Love are you able to comprehend the Truth. This is the law that works unalterably when the energy is being exchanged between the octaves. When you experience fear, doubt, and other imperfect feelings, you will be unable to comprehend the whole perfection of the Divine Truth. On the other hand, if you are able to cultivate this feeling of unconditional Divine Love, you will be able to see tremendous Truth, even in one single phrase. This phrase will mean nothing to the majority of mankind, but for you it will open up the whole fullness of the Divine Truth because you have received the key to open it, namely: the Divine Love in your heart. Therefore, do not strive to cultivate the pursuit of knowledge; strive to cultivate the Divine Love in yourself. Your perfection in God is not possible if you cannot develop this quality of Divine Love within yourselves.

You cannot imagine how quickly and clearly humanity will begin to advance along the Divine Path if you are able to understand the importance of the all-encompassing feeling of Love. Many, if not almost all the tests on your Path can be overcome only with the feeling of Love. When Divine Love leaves you, it can be compared to a serious illness. Nobody will help you with that illness if you do not desire to return to the elevated state of consciousness and to the feeling of all-encompassing Love. The feeling of unconditional Love is what you lack; this is what will be the best remedy for you on the spiritual Path.

It is impossible to feel Love if you are driven by other imperfect feelings — for example, the feeling of fear arises due to the shortage of Love. You are afraid of losing something or you are afraid that someone will harm you, but the reason why you have these fears is because you do not have Love in your heart. Therefore, the best remedy for fear is Love, the Love that is Divine in its essence. If you have Love that is not Divine, then that imperfect feeling can tie you to the object of your affection. You should feel unconditional Love, which is not associated with a particular person but to a more general Love. You should love every being in your world and every being in the Divine world.

When you see too many imperfections in other people, it also means that you lack Love. You cannot notice imperfections and feel Love at the same time. These are incompatible qualities.

In the beginning it will be difficult for you to experience the feeling of unconditional Love. That is because your understanding of love is much too related to human sentiments. Therefore, do not be ashamed if, in the beginning, your love is not perfect.

The strength of your Love is also important. That is because Love is the quality that allows you to act in your world. Strength without Love turns into craftiness and resentment. Therefore, you need to start and do everything in your lives only with the feeling of Love. If you have any personal motive, it makes all your actions imperfect. When you try to do a good deed only with your mind, without hearing the sound of the Divine feeling of Love within you, your deed may lead to a bad result instead of a good outcome.

Remember what Jesus taught you: "By their fruits you will recognize them."[15]

Your actions may be absolutely correct — you may be praying, doing community service, helping others — but no matter what you do, it will lead to poor results. This happens because at the moment when you decided to do something, your intention was not colored with Love. Thus, the fruit, the result of your actions, turned out to be rotten. Therefore, if I were you, I would rather not do anything instead of starting something without the feeling of Love. That is because karma, as the result of your actions, will be negative in this case.

Do you understand how the Law of karma works? Do you understand that more and more subtle aspects of this Law are revealed to you as you advance on your Path? That is why we give

---

[15] By their fruit you will recognize them. (Mathew 7:16).

our Teaching. For those who began reading our Messages very recently and who did not read all Dictations from the beginning but instead began reading the last cycle of the Messages, many things that we are talking about will be unclear.

Once again, I have to make the analogy of an educational institution. When you go to school, first you go to the first grade, and then you transfer to the second and third grades. Only very arrogant people can go straight to the tenth grade and demand to study there. Knowledge cannot fill a vessel if the vessel is not prepared properly. We are responsible for ensuring that you understand the Teaching that we give. That is why we teach you very complex Truths in very simple words; many people become confused by that. It seems to them that everything we say is old truths.

Allow me to note that in this case you are driven by your ego, and the lack of Divine Love will one day play an evil trick on you. That is why we give our Messages based on the feeling of deep, unconditional Love, but you also need to accept the nectar of our Teaching when you are attuned to the Divine tone and filled with Love. I do not recommend that you begin reading our Messages until you reach a balanced state of consciousness. Think about what I said, and try to find the mechanisms in your life that will help you to come into a balanced state of consciousness.

I would recommend that you pay attention to every small detail that surrounds you in your lives. You should maintain tidiness in your house and at your workplace. You should carefully select the food you eat and maintain the cleanliness of your body. Note to yourselves that in addition to physical dirt, you also collect a lot of astral and mental dirt throughout the day. The best way of cleaning yourselves from that dirt will be bathing in a pure natural reservoir or at least taking a shower or a full bath twice daily, in the morning and in the evening.

I was with you on this day to provide guidance regarding everyday life. Do not think that what has been said does not concern each of you individually.

I AM Kuthumi.

A Teaching about the necessity to keep your lower bodies pure

July 4, 2007

I AM Kuthumi, who has come again in order to give another Message to the people of Earth. I have come on this day to remind you about your duty. Many of you, before taking on this incarnation, had received special training at our schools and ashrams located on the Subtle plane.

You attended our classes and prepared for the mission. Many of you, during your adolescent years, still retained subtle recollections about the need to do something for the world. Your hearts were burning with the flame of Service, but nothing around you reminded you about your duty.

Now I have come to remind you about the purpose of your incarnation. All the fuss of life should become secondary. You need to know how to set priorities in your life. There are primary tasks and there are secondary tasks. There are eternal tasks, there are the tasks of the current incarnation, and there is the daily fuss. When you allow the daily fuss to come over you every day, year after year, your sense organs lose the perception of the Subtle plane; you stuff your consciousness with such a great amount of unnecessary information that you are simply unable to seclude yourselves and come into the stillness of our world.

You are very sensitive beings. Your subtle bodies, when attuned to the Higher worlds, are like a Stradivarius violin. However, many of you prefer to drive nails with that violin. Imagine a real Stradivarius violin. Generations of people have been enjoying its charming sounds. You are taught to recognize its value as a true piece of art. Why do you value yourselves less than a violin? You are much better conduits of the energies of the Subtle plane. You are capable of transmitting the energies of the Higher worlds into your world. However, you treat the material things of your world with much greater respect than you treat yourselves.

Your unwillingness to listen to yourselves and keep yourselves in purity is related to your psychological problems, and the lack of love for yourselves lies at the root of these problems of yours. You need to love yourselves, not as a physical body but as the manifestation of God on Earth. You are a part of God, and you should take care of all your bodies and maintain them purely as a manifestation of the Divine.

All your bodies need proper care. Your physical body must receive proper nutrition. The higher the vibrations of the food, the less food you need to eat.

Your emotional body needs food in the form of the subtle energies that come from the Higher worlds. Your emotional body constantly needs to be recharged with the subtle energy. You try to satisfy the hunger of your emotional body by feeding it with surrogates consisting of low-quality music and television programs. You litter your emotional body by constantly putting it in the unfavorable conditions that exist in your world. Try to protect yourselves from the sounds that come from all directions. One hour a day of listening to the radio or watching television is enough to deprive you of communication with the Higher worlds for one month.

Think about what you surround yourselves with in your lives. The vibrations of it all are so distant from those of our world.

One shot of alcohol that you drink or one cigarette that you smoke does not allow you to rise to the Higher etheric octaves for several days. You are forced to constantly reside at the levels of the astral plane because you have tied yourselves to it, like using ropes, by your harmful habits.

Carefully analyze what you load your mental body with. How much time do you spend watching endless soap operas and in conversations with people? Do not be afraid to be left alone with yourself. Learn how to listen to the silence and enjoy the solitude.

Legislative measures should be taken toward those who are trying to upset the world with the sounds of ragged rhythms. Each of those who like to listen to rock music, or to any kind of music with improper rhythms, lowers the vibration of the surrounding space for many miles around. This hooliganism must be stopped.

While the alcohol that you drink and the cigarettes that you smoke lower only your own vibrations and the vibrations of the people who live with you, the pounding music affects thousands of people. If you knew about the consequences of such hooliganism for your lower bodies, the first thing you would do would be to prohibit your children from listening to such music forever.

There are very simple measures that allow you to quickly raise the vibrations on the physical plane, and one of these measures is the prohibition of listening to loud music.

You cannot even imagine what influence music has on you. Every night I come to my organ, and inspired by God, I play charming melodies. There are a very small number of people who come to my retreat to listen to this music. Even a smaller number of people are capable of reproducing that music in their awakened state of consciousness, writing it down with notes, and presenting it to the world.

Oh, how I wish that the consonance with the Higher world to be accessible to you through listening to the music that I play on my organ.

If during the day you have been under the influence of your horrible music, even if you heard it only briefly on public transportation or at a store, then that night you will no longer be able to rise to the octaves where my organ is heard.

You limit yourselves. You should remember your mission and take all the necessary measures to purify yourselves to such an extent that you are able to fulfill your mission, for the sake of which you have taken on this incarnation. You have forgotten everything, and you yourselves are guilty of this forgetfulness because you do not pay proper attention to taking care of your four lower bodies.

Think about how much simpler it would be for the next generation to fulfill their missions if you had already started to consider creating the places on Earth now, where the new generation could incarnate and spend their first years of life in stillness and in association with nature. If such places on Earth were created now, then a new race of people would be able to come into incarnation. Believe me; many advanced souls are ready to incarnate in order to give their Service to the world. Only the lack of arranged conditions on the physical plane makes them postpone their incarnation for years, and even decades.

Many of the high spirits take on the risk and incarnate in unprepared conditions. What do you think happens? Right after birth, they are compelled to burden themselves with such a large amount of karma, which they take from the people who surround them by absorbing that karma into their auras, that by the age of four these unique children are unable to reveal their abilities and serving the world until the end of their incarnation.

It is painful for us to see how the best sons and daughters of mankind perish among you while carrying your burden and dying under its load.

Have you never heard or read everything that I told you today? How many times do you need to hear these simple truths in order to put them into practice?

I am ready to come to you as many times as needed for you to master my Teaching. However, your progress will be better if before going to sleep you desire to come to that hall on the etheric plane where I play my organ and if throughout the day you try to protect yourselves from everything that may prevent you from hearing my organ.

I AM Kuthumi, loving you always.

A Teaching on the liberation from karma

January 7, 2008

I AM Kuthumi, who has come to instruct your souls. I have come today to give a small Teaching that I hope will be very useful for you and will lead you to a better understanding of many things. I am keeping the immaculate concept of each of you. This makes it easy for me to talk to you and to see how my attitude toward you affects your lives.

Have you ever noticed what impact you have on other people, those who are known to you (friends, relatives, and children) or strangers? Have you ever watched yourself as if from the outside?

Now, you are not in a good mood. You are imbued with suspicion and hostility. You think that everybody deceives you and treats you badly. After all, you have experienced such states in your lives, haven't you? Now let us carefully analyze how this state of yours affects everything that surrounds you.

So, you come to your work place and you begin to shift your state onto the people around you. You think not very good things about them. Gradually, people automatically read your vibrations and turn to you the side that you see in them. Do you know what I mean by that? Initially, there is low-quality energy within you that leads to your inferior inner state. Your mental and emotional bodies begin to vibrate at the frequency that corresponds to the low energy that is activated within you at this moment.

You know that your energy bodies contain all the records of the deeds you have previously performed. Then the moment comes when this or that karmic record is activated. Thus, you find yourself in the state of consciousness that you previously created by your wrong choices in the past.

So, there comes the moment again when you are faced with the low-quality energy that you have created yourself and that lives in your energy bodies. Now it depends only on you whether you will be able to work off this energy, to balance and neutralize it, or you will worsen your karmic state.

When you are equipped with the knowledge about the operation of the Law of Karma, you can learn to capture all the inferior states that begin to manifest within you. You will gradually master the art of observing how a particular inferior state arises, becomes activated, and penetrates into your mental and emotional bodies. Then, when you know your enemy, you can overcome it.

If you know your disease, you can take the medicine in time and the attack will be prevented. Your subtle bodies are also sick, and they contain the wounds from your past wrong actions. You just need to find an antidote or a remedy for your inferior states of consciousness. You should learn to capture the moment when the inferior state of consciousness is just beginning to take hold of you. You must be alert, and exactly at that point you must stop any manifestations of your past negative energies.

If you try to cope with your inferior state by force of will or by using some psychological techniques, it will be unlikely to help you. You need to understand that you yourselves created this state in the past, and now you intend to get rid of this imperfection and let it go.

When you manage to come into a higher state of consciousness and turn the flow of the Divine energy within you in the right direction, you will be able to neutralize your past negative karmic deposits.

The whole mechanism of correcting your inner imperfections lies within you. You only need to acknowledge that these imperfections are present inside of you and wish to become free from them.

Everything depends on the severity of your karma and on the strength of this negative energy settling within you. If you are dealing with a small karmic problem, it is enough for you to fix your attention on this problem once, and it will leave you.

If you encounter a big karmic problem, the quality or trait that you have come into incarnation to work off, you will have to repeat your experience many times, sometimes for several years.

There is no such negative quality or fault that cannot be surmounted with the help of God.

God always gives you an opportunity to cope with any of your faults independently.

When you feel that the recommendations being given to you by me work flawlessly, you can gradually get rid of all your imperfections.

The day will come and you will no longer be offended, if previously resentment was inherent in you.

The day will come and you will no longer be envious, if you were envious.

The day will come and you will no longer be jealous, if you were jealous.

Similarly, you can get rid of depression, irritability, quick temper, anger, and many other non-divine qualities.

Then, when you are able to manifest only Divine qualities, the whole world will turn its Divine side toward you.

Each one of you needs to deal only with yourself, only with your own inner state, and the world around you will change by itself.

I was a little bit cunning when I was giving you this Teaching. Actually, all of you are interconnected in your world. There are very strong karmic bonds that bind you to your families, your countries, and the whole planet. Therefore, simultaneously with the process of purifying yourselves from the karmic deposits and layers, you should show concern for other people so that they can also become aware of the Law of Karma and how they can work off their karma.

After the knowledge of the Law of Karma and the methods of working off the karma penetrate into the consciousness of a critical percentage of the people on Earth, the situation on the planet will begin to change right before your eyes.

Your ignorance and laziness often impede you. All the mechanisms and all the knowledge were given to you long ago, both in the Dictations that we give through this Messenger and through many other people who have served us as our Messengers at different times.

Now the time has come for us to part. It is a pity.

I look forward to our new meetings in the future.

I AM Kuthumi,
the instructor of your souls.

A Teaching on changing of vibrations

January 2, 2009

I AM Kuthumi, who has come to you on this day in order to give a Teaching that may seem new to you; however, we taught this subject to our disciples back in the temples of ancient Lemuria.

This Teaching is related to how you lose the attunement with the Divinity in your lives and how you can regain the attunement with the Divine world.

The entire mechanism of how it happens is hidden within you. Therefore, you do not need to go to any priests, witchdoctors, healers, and especially physicians in order to find this mechanism in you — the ability to instantly raise the level of your vibrations within minutes and to rise to the level of etheric octaves. I have probably intrigued you very much.

Nevertheless, I insist that each of you is able to elevate your consciousness during the day by yourself, without any outside help, even when you are in the unfavorable environment of a city or a smaller town.

There have always been temples, separate halls where one could abstract oneself from the hustle and tune into Eternity.

Now, even the temples are filled with the same hustle as there is in the streets. That is why the only place where you can feel comfortable and where you can come in contact with Eternity is inside your heart.

There, inside of you, the worlds come together. There, inside of you, you are able to gain peace even when the storms of your time are knocking you down.

You should acquire this skill. This skill is developed. First of all, you should understand that your being is multifaceted and multidimensional. You have come into the physical world in order to gain experience. For that, you are given the armor — your physical body. When you understand that your physical body is not your real part, you instantly rise in your consciousness to the level of the Higher etheric octaves.

This is a very simple practice that does not require any additional actions or preparations from you. All you need to do in order to learn this practice is to constantly exercise it. When you are an athlete and you want to achieve a record, even a world-record result in your sport, you devote all your life to attaining this.

Therefore, in order for you to learn how to elevate your consciousness in a matter of minutes, you should also practice this science, and the result will not be long in coming.

It may seem to you that this is a very abstract practice and that, most likely, it will not be of any use to you in your reality.

Do not jump to conclusions. Imagine that you find yourselves in an environment that is burning with human passions and that you are also getting involved in this process. Then, while you are still maintaining control over yourself, you remember your practice of quick elevation of vibrations, and you begin to concentrate on your real part. What happens outside of you? All the storms and negative energies are left below the level of your consciousness and do not touch you. You become invisible to those people who have just ranted and raved against you. It becomes uninteresting for them to continue their exercises, and they either calm down or turn their attention to another subject.

Of course, I have slightly exaggerated the description of the situation regarding the leap of consciousness. In reality, in order to constantly change the level of your consciousness, you need a very serious preparation of all your bodies. All of your bodies must be able to withstand the pressure in a very wide range of vibrations. Then the leap will become a reality for you. The majority of people are vibrating within a very limited range of frequencies. Many of them do not even notice what is happening literally under their noses if it belongs to higher vibrations.

For a person who is able to broaden his or her consciousness and capture several adjacent vibrational octaves, both the physical and the Subtle worlds become available. The practice of acquiring spatial vibrations was one of the main practices in the schools of initiations of the past. When the disciples were able to withstand totally opposite vibrations for a short period of time, it was considered that they had achieved the level of initiations where they themselves could teach such a method to others.

The fact is that in order to achieve an instant switch of vibrations of all bodies from the lowest level to the highest, and vice versa, all bodies must be prepared for it. None of the bodies must be burdened with an extra load. Then all the bodies will run down the mountain in seconds and also climb the mountain in seconds. I am saying that none of the bodies — the physical, astral, mental and etheric — should be burdened with karma.

You should have no extraneous thoughts, no foul feelings, and no toxins in the physical body.

When the bodies are ready for such overstrain, a person becomes initiated.

Of course, a long time is necessary in order for people to be able to control themselves at different vibrational levels and to consciously switch between these levels.

Your time gives you the opportunity to master the practice of instantly changing vibrations without stepping away from your everyday life.

Just do not forget that in order to master this technique, you will have to change your lifestyle and devote your life to only one task: the Service to all living beings. This is because if your motive for acquiring this method is, for example, to achieve personal superiority, then a block will appear in your mental body and in the body of desire, and it will not allow you to travel to different vibrational levels.

The next stage is the stage of instant repositioning in space. However, it seems to me that it will be enough for you for now to acquire the more simple method that I have described in today's talk.

I will be happy to meet in the etheric octaves of Light with those who achieve success.

I AM Kuthumi.

A Talk of vital importance

July 2, 2009

I AM Kuthumi. I have come to hold discourse.

I would like to talk to you openly, honestly, and directly.

My heart wishes to talk to you about many things but above all, of course, about something that is of the most interest and the most value for you at this stage.

The confusion that is present in your world is, of course, primarily caused by you yourselves. First, you perform irresponsible deeds and allow imperfect thoughts and feelings to seize hold of your being, and then you are astonished at the effects caused by your actions, thoughts, and feelings.

The mental field of the planet is overloaded with your negative states of consciousness. The same thing takes place on the astral plane.

You hardly ever think about the impact that your thoughts and feelings have on everything that surrounds you. In fact, all the negative effects that are present in nature, in weather conditions, in the financial sphere, and in any other spheres of life on planet Earth are generated by you yourselves. After some time, your own fruits materialize in the physical plane of planet Earth in the form of hurricanes, showers, droughts, or floods.

Many times we talked about the direct and immediate link that exists between your state of consciousness and everything that happens on planet Earth.

Your forgetfulness and constant hope that things will somehow become right by themselves make us, the Ascended Masters, doubt whether humanity is at all able to hear us and perceive the information that we give.

It has been said dozens of times that it is necessary to watch your thoughts and feelings, it is necessary to dedicate attention to the analysis of everything that happens to you during the day. It is just impossible to provide clearer signs on the physical plane. The next step is going to be a catastrophe of such magnitude that you can imagine but are afraid to even think about it.

Why do you read our Messages if you do not act according to our instructions and requests in your lives? It seems that humanity has come to the stage of its development when it is no longer able to adequately respond to the information.

In my Dictations, I have personally told you many times that you suffer from an excess of information. You overload your minds with various pieces of news and information that comes to you from different sources to such an extent that you have become not only incapable of discerning true information from false, but now you do not react to any information. You just let it pass by, and everything that flows into your consciousness during the day cannot stay there for a minute. The defense mechanism gets activated.

That is why I have come today to tell you one more time that you have to approach any information that you get very carefully. Even when it seems to you that the information passes by your consciousness, it has an ability to settle in your subconscious minds. And you can never tell when and what kind of influence your subconscious minds will exert on you, your choices, and your behavior.

The genie of permissiveness and accessibility of any information has been let out of the bottle. And the only way out of this situation is to protect yourselves against everything that is unnecessary for your evolutionary development. If you do not take steps in that direction, then the next generation will not be able to respond adequately to any information at all. Constant repetition influences your consciousness as coding. That is why you should expose yourselves to the influence of modern mass media with great caution. The time has come when you have to separate the wheat from the chaff in everything that surrounds you, and reject everything that is not Divine. I understand that when you are under constant pressure from all the modern, advanced technologies bombarding your consciousness at full power, 24 hours a day through hundreds of television and radio channels, it is hard for you to find your bearings and understand how to act in this situation.

We teach you discernment and the right choices that you can make. And the first and most reasonable thing is to limit the influence of all the mass media on your consciousness and subconsciousness. When that pressure lessens, you will gain an ability to navigate and to make the distinction. Your Higher Self, God within you, cannot talk to you; the Ascended Masters cannot talk to you while you are sealed off in the tons of informational trash that are poured out on you during the day from TV screens, radios, newspapers, and the Internet. You get a feeling that you are well-informed about all the latest events of the world, that you get information about all the innovations in all spheres. However, the most important news that is not broadcast on any of your radio or TV channels is not available for most of the people of Earth. The main news is the SOS signal that your planet and everything that lives on it is sending.

You are like a mad captain who navigates a ship in a storm. The collective consciousness and the collective subconscious of humanity are like this mad captain. And at any moment the ship — your planet — may strike sharp reefs and be shipwrecked.

You have tried; you have tasted all the fruits on planet Earth, and now the time has come when it is necessary to get back to more subtle manifestations of existence. How can you hear the sounds of music from my organ that I play every night in my retreat in the etheric octaves if you continuously deafen yourselves with all the background noise from your loud equipment?

Listening to silence, to the living voices of nature, is tiresome and boring for you. You have created an artificial civilization that has torn itself from everything that God created on planet Earth.

I have come in order to try one more time to deliver the simple truths to your consciousness. And I become silent in the hope that all of you have heard me.

I AM Kuthumi.

A Teaching on the liberation from negative energies

December 12, 2009

I AM Kuthumi.

Perhaps those of you who regularly read our Messages that we give through our Messenger will remember me. I come often, and my talks mainly concern the development of your consciousness. I also specialize in solving psychological problems with which your souls are burdened.

Today I would like to devote time to a talk about where your psychological problems come from and whether it is possible for you to free yourselves from them without the help of psychotherapists. It should be said that the Ascended Masters and human psychotherapists approach the liberation from psychological problems differently. Human psychotherapists use the terms "subconscious" and "unconscious," whereas I usually use the terms "soul" and "subtle bodies."

This would not be a big difference if your specialists approached you not as clients and sources of their subsistence in the physical world but as souls that need help and support.

I have to state the deplorable fact that practically all people living on planet Earth now are in need of help. And I mean help in solving psychological problems that are burdening their souls and pass from embodiment to embodiment. Many specialists and psychotherapists reject the fact that the soul has a very ancient history and passes through many incarnations. And this makes it impossible to fully help many souls who need help. Many problems came to them from their previous embodiments: various fears, phobias, and death records. Many souls are burdened with these problems and do not know how to free themselves from them.

I will not give you a universal prescription. I can only give you my own advice and recommendations. And I will be glad if you manage to use these recommendations in your lives. I will be even happier if my recommendations bring healing to your souls.

First, you need to realize that the problem is in you and burdens your subtle bodies. For example, this can be hatred toward the opposite sex, which originated from an experience in your past. In your current embodiment, you have a beautiful family and there is no cause for the manifestation of hatred and enmity. But you can do nothing with yourself. From time to time you experience attacks of hatred or anger. You suffer from this yourself, and it also affects the people close to you: your spouse and your children.

The first and most important step to solving your problem is the recognition of the fact that this problem exists within you. This is a very big and vital step. When you read these lines, it may seem funny to you that you cannot recognize such a problem. Do not jump to conclusions. You can see this problem in other people, but when the karmic energy of hatred and enmity rises within yourself, when it overwhelms you and totally flows over you like an ocean wave, you cannot evaluate the situation rationally. Your anger seems fully justified to you, and you find, or rather your carnal mind finds, a thousand satisfactory excuses for your state, your behavior, and your actions.

When this horrible, negative energy from your past embodiments rises within you, it is very difficult for you to cope with yourself. You do not know how many times in your past incarnations you experienced the most severe treatment from the opposite sex. You could have been humiliated, beaten up, and even violated and killed. The records of all these negative experiences are lying in your subtle bodies as a burden. And your task, your foremost task, is to try to realize that this energy, this negative energy, is present within you.

It is not your husband or wife that is the cause of your negative state of consciousness but the energy that exists within you. The complexity of the situation is that most likely within your husband or wife, there is also an energy that needs to be worked off. And, most probably, while under the influence of negative energy you blame your husband, for example, for some actions or thoughts that he does not have in the current embodiment; it was just in his previous embodiments he allowed himself to perform the precise actions you reproach him for. Therefore, the process of healing from low-quality energies becomes more complicated because this is a mutual process. You can render help to each other to free yourselves from the negative energies. You just need to agree between yourselves that when this negative energy is rising in one of you, the other must signal that here it is, this energy has risen. And then, helping each other, you will become aware of the presence of this energy within you. And you will be able to separate this energy from yourself.

You will become able to realize that this is the part of you that you wish to free yourself from.

The second vital step comes when you manage to recognize the presence of the negative energy that exists within you, and you begin to feel an impulse to get rid of that negative energy.

The next step is the easiest one. You ask God to liberate you from the negative energy that is present in you. But, with all its seeming simplicity, this step cannot be done by everybody. Usually, people are very mobile in their consciousness. They are able to ask God once or twice to free them from the negative energy, but then they forget about their appeal and about their decision to get rid of the negative energy. Then, when the next karmic moment comes and the negative energy totally overwhelms them again, people are puzzled. Why didn't God free them from this energy?

This, beloved, is because the negative energy that is present in you has sometimes been formed throughout the entire previous embodiment or during several embodiments. That is why you should go to great lengths to become free from this energy. You may involve prayer practice; you may use the dispensation on the 23rd of each month[16] that was

---

[16] More information about the dispensation of the 23rd can be found in these Dictations: "The best sermon will be your personal example," Goddess of Liberty, April 22, 2005; "About the opportunity to unburden your karma of the next month and about the letters to the Karmic Board," Beloved Surya, June 23, 2005; "About the new Divine dispensation," Beloved El Morya, June 27, 2005; "I have brought you two pieces of news — one

described in detail in a series of Dictations through this Messenger. You may use the dispensation of writing letters to the Karmic Board[17] that was also given to you in detail.

Sometimes only your everyday endeavors during a number of years can help you to free yourself from the negative energies of the past.

The negative qualities that you acquired during the current embodiment are worked off much more easily, but the qualities that accompany you from embodiment to embodiment require a lot of effort to be worked off.

Many qualities can be worked off through the direct interaction with your spouses. Day after day, you face each other's negative qualities, and you realize that these are the negative energies that you

---

is sad and the other one is joyful," Beloved El Morya, January 7, 2006; "About the forthcoming day of the summer solstice and the Divine favors connected with this day," Lord Maitreya, June 15, 2006; "About the dispensation of the 23rd and other opportunities being given by Heaven," Beloved El Morya, July 19, 2006; "One more vital point is added to the dispensation on the 23rd of each month," Gautama Buddha, December 25, 2006. Refer to *Words of Wisdom, Volume I and Volume II.*

[17] The Karmic Board meeting is held twice a year for two weeks beginning at the time of the summer or the winter solstice. Refer to the Dictation "About the opportunity to unburden your karma of the next month and about the letters to the Karmic Board," Beloved Surya, June 23, 2005 in *Words of Wisdom, Volume I.*

need to free yourself from, and you forgive each other and help each other throughout your lives.

Only this way, by helping each other, are you sometimes able to overcome the karma of the past. And the main element that can help you in dissolving the past karma is the love that you feel toward each other. This is the greatest treasure of your world, which is worth cherishing and protecting much more than money, things, or gold.

I am glad that our talk has taken place today.

**I AM Kuthumi,
with Love to you and your souls.**

A Talk about the effect of the Messages

January 14, 2010

I AM Kuthumi. I have come to you again. Today we will continue our discussion about overcoming the inner qualities that impede you.

Yes, beloved, unfortunately, you live in a world that is not perfect; consequently, you have to share the imperfections of this world. That is why it is often difficult for you to understand very simple things that we talk about. And many of you are even perplexed about what is new in our talks and how much longer we will be talking about the same things.

Your consciousness is designed in such a way that, in order for any changes in your consciousness to really occur, you have to hear the same truth many times. And even when it seems to you that you already know this truth, you still have to make your own efforts so that you not only understand this truth but also implement it in your lives.

Trust me and my experience in working with humankind of Earth. And even if it seems to you that you are not getting anything new from our Messages, do not jump to conclusions.

We regularly repeat our recommendations about how to work with our Messages. And I know many people who do not follow our recommendations. We have talked many times about being careful when working with the Messages and that it is not recommended to read more than two Messages per day. For example, one Message can be read in the morning, and one in the evening.

Each Message contains energies of the various Masters who transmit these Messages. And sometimes the energies do not belong to a very high plane, while other times the energies belong to a very high plane of Existence. And if you start reading several Messages in a row, you put your body under great pressure. Your outer consciousness may not detect this danger, because your carnal mind is used to dealing with just the informational component, and it does not take into consideration the energy component of the Messages.

I will give you an example. Your body needs food. And when you are hungry or thirsty and you eat a slice of bread or drink a glass of pure water, your body feels satisfied.

Now imagine if you were eating a lot of different kinds of food, without any boundaries, and consuming an unlimited amount of different drinks. I know that many of you do this in your lives, indulge in abundant feasts and gluttony. But don't you feel ill the next day after you have eaten or drunk too much?

There are foods that can be combined with each other, whereas there are foods that cannot be consumed simultaneously. But the majority of people are at such a low energy level that they are unable to understand these simple truths that have been known for thousands of years and followed by all wise men.

When you read a lot of Dictations from different Masters, you may get the same indigestion in your consciousness, just like the indigestion you get in your stomach from uncontrolled food consumption.

You should approach the reading of our Messages very carefully or you might experience inner discomfort or dissatisfaction. Worse yet, you might direct all your displeasure at our Messenger or the Masters.

You should prepare yourself for reading each Message very carefully. You should attune yourself to the Master who is giving the Message with the help of music, the image of the Master, or using a prayer or meditation before reading the Message.

That way, you are balancing your energy, elevating your consciousness, and the Messages will be beneficial to you.

I will give you another example. The sun is shining on all people and all living beings. And there are people who are using the solar energy wisely. They spend some time in the sun, take a break, and then they expose themselves again to the caressing sunbeams.

There is another group of people who spend all day at the beach under the burning sun and then suffer from burns and fever the next day.

Who is to blame for their sunburn? Is it the sun? I think that the answer is obvious. It is their own fault that they have excessively used the sun's energy.

The energy that our Messages contain does not have such obvious effects, but there are still a considerable number of individuals who briefly look through a dozen or so of our Messages without getting to the essence and without attuning themselves properly before reading each Message. The result comes quickly. After a certain period of time, they begin to feel irritated and even angry.

Who is at fault that you are experiencing these feelings? The Messenger? The Masters? I think that the answer is obvious. Nobody outside of you is to blame for neglecting the recommendations of the Masters.

Like everything in your world, our Messages have a dual effect. And thanks to our Messages, some people have attained smoothness of their auras, and the imperfections of their auras that they had had for many years have disappeared. They have become more balanced and friendly. Their relationships with family have improved. And peace has come to their souls and homes.

However, others, on the contrary, experience anger, hatred, and disaffection after reading our Messages. Their auras are dissolving day after day, and they are simply destroying themselves.

Beloved, we are wishing you kindness, Love, and harmony. And you can obtain all this thanks to our Messages. But, inside of you there is a valve that directs the energy contained in our Messages, either for good or for evil. Everything in your world, beloved, has a dual effect. And inside of you there is a mechanism that either makes you vigorously follow the path of evolution or throws you off to the roadside.

Today I have had the opportunity to hold a very important talk. I hope that for many people who read our Messages, this talk will be more than topical.

I AM Kuthumi,
always ready to help anyone who is in
need of help and who is asking for help.

A Teaching on vibrations and the interconnection of everything that exists on Earth

June 12, 2010

I AM Kuthumi.

I hope that our talk today will be informative for you and will make you see the things you are used to observing around you in another way. I will try to provide you with an insight that is as close as possible to the view that the Ascended Masters have of what is around you, as well as the current situation in the world.

I feel that I have intrigued you. In many of our Messages, we constantly talk about the vibrations and about the need to raise those vibrations. That abstract assertion has a very concrete manifestation in your physical world. And if you made the effort to be more inquisitive, then you would find out that the data of your secular science have deciphered the phenomenon of raising the vibrations long ago.

If the results of the scientific research became widely known, then this would inevitably lead to an explosion in your consciousness. So, you are intrigued even more, aren't you?

I affirm that many scientists of the world have at their disposal the data concerning how the vibrations of human cells change under the influence of the lifestyles that humans lead. These vibrations impact human health, particularly the organs and systems.

Everything can be measured. And everything has a scientific explanation. I myself participated in the transmission of many scientific discoveries into your world, working with biologists and biophysicists.

The vibrations of your cells vary greatly depending on the food you eat, the conditions you live in, whether you have any addictions, and even whether you are inclined to listen to music containing disharmonious vibrations. Living in large cities leads to a sharp decrease in the vibrations of cells. Therefore, no matter how you try to reach the next stage of evolutionary development while living in big cities, you will not succeed. The urban infrastructure is capable of producing a low-frequency rumble that extends hundreds of miles around big cities and dozens of miles around smaller towns.

Therefore, the spiritual achievements that you allegedly have, living in large cities, only provoke our smiles. You have to be very ignorant and completely unaware of the mechanism of spiritual processes to dare allege that your spiritual level is high while you live in any big city.

Living in a city makes it impossible to raise the vibrations of your cells, even if you lead a righteous way of living, you do not smoke, you do not consume alcohol and drugs, you do not eat meat, and you do not listen to rock music. Everything is interconnected in your world, and you are a unified system with everything that surrounds you. Therefore, your cells cannot have vibrations higher than the allowed maximum of the vibrations of the city. And this level of vibrations can be measured.

When you move to a clean and quiet place, the vibrations of your cells increase and you get an opportunity for spiritual growth and advancement. I am talking about true spiritual advancement.

You may think that all the efforts you make for spiritual growth while living in big cities are in vain. Nothing is in vain. You cannot immediately reach those vibrations that are inherent in the hermits in Tibet. Your organs and systems will not be able to withstand that. But advancing gradually along the spiritual path, you will notice that continuing to live in large cities will become impossible for you, and you will more and more resemble a fish cast out on the shore.

Everything can be changed, but it is necessary to know what to aim for and how to achieve it. As a whole, society is not ready to accept these simple truths that I am telling you. Therefore, we can only wait until you ripen and become ready for the next stage of evolutionary development.

It is necessary for you to change your way of living. It is necessary for you to change your habits. It is necessary for you to change your consumer attitude toward nature.

A person with low vibrations creates conditions for millions of parasites to live within him or her. And the population of Earth is almost completely full of parasites. That is the cause of illnesses, lack of strength, and the desire to live.

Do you know what the reason for your condition is? It is your attitude toward nature, toward all Life, toward everything that exists together with you on Earth. The Law functions wisely. Your parasitic attitude toward Earth and nature causes a predominance of parasites in your organism. And exactly as you can get rid of the parasites inside of you with cleansing procedures, in the same way Earth will eventually be forced to conduct cleansing procedures. And you alone are to blame when, after consecutive disasters, those individuals who are not ready to part with the parasitic status of their consciousness will be washed off the face of Earth.

The next stage of evolution presupposes sensible cooperation with Earth and with everything that exists on it. However, you will need to work off the karma — karma that has accumulated by the rapacious and barbarian attitude toward nature — with illnesses, cataclysms, and man-made catastrophes.

The burden of the return of karma can be regulated by more and more individuals ascending to a new level of consciousness; they will then be capable of realizing the oneness of all Life.

Now you are at a critical point. And humanity has been balancing at this point of its development for two hundred years. Each time our intervention helped to postpone the unfavorable development of events. However, today I came with a specific purpose to give you the keys so you can overcome the crisis in your consciousness as painlessly as possible.

Otherwise, more and more often, you will have to hear in the news that consecutive cataclysms are taking place here and there. Here and there, entire cities and continents are washed off the face of Earth. And you will get used to it, and it will seem to you that it is natural and that it has always been this way.

The memory of humanity is very weak. And many do not even remember what happened yesterday, not to mention a longer period of time.

In order not to part with you on a sad note, I am inclined to tell you that there is a probability of a favorable development of events on Earth. However, this probability can be realized only with the help of humankind.

I AM Kuthumi.

Today's talk will explain to you the failures on your Path

December 28, 2010

I AM Kuthumi, having come again in order to have a talk with you.

Perhaps you will benefit from what I want to tell you. At least, it will be useful for the development of your souls.

As we have already mentioned in our Messages several times, there is something in every person that is truly a real treasure. And this treasure has the ability to increase from incarnation to incarnation or to vanish completely. It is like you were robbed. And this is indeed a complete analogy. But the fact is that you rob yourself.

Perhaps, I am speaking in riddles, and my previous phrases require interpretation. As you should have understood from our previous talks, within a person there is an immortal part and there is a perishable, impermanent part. And all the radiant experiences of many incarnations are accumulated like treasures in Heaven in your causal body, an imperishable part of you.

However, if incarnation after incarnation, a person wastes the Divine energy coming through a crystal string, not on Divine acts but giving to himself the pleasures of life and fulfilling the desires of his ego, then the treasures are not accumulated. In fact, you rob yourself.

Every incarnated person is given a certain amount of energy. And you control that energy yourself. So in fact, there is not any Last Judgment at the end of the cosmic cycles. But the people who incorrectly spent the energy given by God (from the Divine point of view) just cannot continue their existence because there is nothing to evolve further.

This is the Teaching, its main essence that we try to convey to the consciousness of human individuals.

Every time, when reading the lines of the Teaching, a person heeds them but then in the next moment they rush in pursuit of the next pleasure or to fulfill a desire.

This inconsistency in actions and forgetfulness make us repeat the same Truths many times.

At first glance, it seems that we are doing a useless thing. However, if only one person suddenly awakens and completely realizes the Truth during one of our talks, then the energy for the transmission of our Messages will not be wasted.

While moving along the path of evolution, the illusion becomes increasingly refined, and many things that did not take place in the last centuries are now beginning to manifest. Yes, while moving along the path, our disciples face more and more subtle manifestations of illusion both within themselves as well as outside.

Just take the discovery made by some people and concerning the fact that even when working for the Brotherhood's missions, it turns out, it is possible to create karma.

From the point of view of many people, this statement seems absurd. But let us examine that justification with a concrete example.

A person has started performing a certain job for the Brotherhood: distributing books, giving lectures, translating Messages into other languages, and so on. And he has been doing that job for many years. It seems that in this case the Law of Karma should be satisfied and the person should get his reward in the growth of his causal body.

However, in more than 90 percent of the cases, there is not any growth in the causal body, and moreover, karma is created.

I think that most of the readers will think that something is confused in the text when they read these lines.

There is nothing wrong in the text. It is just that some of our chelas take on certain duties and think that they will carry those duties through their lives like rewards and that it is enough to satisfy the Divine Law. However, it is not the performance of the job itself that is an achievement (even the work for the Brotherhood) but the quality of the performance of this work. You must perform the work of the Brotherhood in such a way that you forget about yourself and forget about everything in the world until you fulfill everything in the best possible way. You cannot perform the work of the Brotherhood in a measured and planned way as you would perform any other work in the physical world, because the fruit of your efforts will very quickly manifest itself as rotten fruit on the physical plane if you do not direct your efforts correctly and you are not in the right state of consciousness.

Sometimes it would be better for you not to do the work of the Brotherhood than to do it without the proper state of consciousness and the necessary zeal.

Perhaps you need to return to the prayer practice and work on yourself, your faults, and your psychological problems. Because in order to do the work for the Brotherhood, you should have the spiritual foundation in your past lives. The great saints of the past can be collaborators of the Brotherhood who are able to do the work for the Brotherhood on the physical plane. And it is quite seldom that within one incarnation you will be able to beg God for the opportunity to do the work for the Brotherhood.

As for you, the less your spiritual achievements are and the bigger your ego is, the more quickly you grasp the fulfillment of the jobs of the Brotherhood. That is why mutual claims and dissatisfaction appear. You should understand your level of development. You should feel awe at the slightest possibility of Service that the Masters give you.

I am actually confused by the fact that I am compelled to explain such simple truths that are very well known in the East, but the consciousness of a Western person is hardly able to accommodate it.

I hope today's talk will explain to you the failures on your Path and will make you take the proper place in the line for the right to be collaborators of the Brotherhood.

We open the shortest way to Heaven for our collaborators, but you should agree that it is necessary to sacrifice something in return. And of course, this is your ego, your attachments, habits, lovely hobbies, and psychological problems that stretch from your distant past.

However, I am an optimist by nature. And I hope that if not within this decade then maybe in the next one, our Messages will have the effect that we expected.

I AM Kuthumi, always with hope.

You create your future and the future of the whole planet at the moment of conception of your child

June 17, 2011

I AM Kuthumi, having come to you to give a discourse that will be useful for your souls.

Today we are going to talk about the concerns that are very close and understandable to everyone. More specifically, we are going to talk about your future — about your children, and about the generation of people that will replace you.

By human standards a short period of time will pass, and a new generation of people will replace the generation that is living now. And each successive generation should be better than the previous one. However, this does not always happen. Why? Perhaps many of you wondered why your children are different from you. Why are they impudent, disobedient, and guided in their lives by completely different principles from those you were guided by in your time? What is the reason for this?

I will approach this subject from a standpoint that is probably unexpected for you. I will ask you to remember the period of time that preceded the moment when your child was born. There is no need to share this memory with anyone. Just try to recollect how it happened that a baby was born to you.

Perhaps you will remember that you accidentally discovered that you will have a baby. You might have even been sad or vexed by that fact. Maybe you had not even planned to have a baby and yet he emerged.

What were you thinking about when enjoying a love affair with your partner? I suppose that most of you were not thinking about creating a new human being who was to come to this world and become a creator of this world.

Your energy flows where your attention is directed. You were thinking about getting pleasure for yourself or for your sex partner, weren't you? Thus, the precious Divine energy was directed at getting pleasure.

But the Divine Will played a trick on you and a baby appeared. What did your child get in this case? What part of the Divine energy?

You yourself disposed of the Divine energy and directed it to getting pleasure. What, from that precious energy, did a new being who was so eager to get into your world receive?

You supplied your child with only the residual amount of the Divine energy. That is, the entire Divine energy boost that was supposed to accompany your child throughout all his life remained on the things around you when you were seeking pleasures.

I think now you remember that moment.

Some of you may say that you were expecting a baby and praying for his or her birth. And indeed, your child was long expected and welcomed by you. But remember those days of your youth that preceded your child's birth.

You wanted to get sexual pleasure, and you experimented with your sexual energy. You did many things that you are even ashamed to remember. And every time you got pleasure you wasted your sexual potential, which was required for your child's birth so that your child would be healthy not only physically but also mentally. And when you settled down and were looking forward to the conception of your long-awaited first-born child, do you think that he received much of the Divine energy? Didn't you supply your child only with the residual amount?

If your sexual pleasures were wild and indecent, what soul do you think you can attract as your child? Everything is attracted according to vibrations. And, the soul you will attract as your first-born child will be attracted to you after you have burdened yourself with a significant amount of karma accumulated while satisfying your desires.

After your reflection, have you come to realize that you yourselves are to blame for all the problems of the next generation of people on planet Earth?

You cannot say that you have nothing to do with the fact that every new generation is less and less viable than the previous one.

Therefore, in order to change the situation on the planet, we come and give our Teaching. You should be clearly aware of the connection between your actions and the consequences of your actions.

Only when you learn to control your desires, thoughts, and feelings, will you be able to gradually overcome the karma of your past wrong choices and deeds.

However, I must warn you about another mistake. Many of you are inclined to blame yourselves for those improper deeds that you performed in your youth. And sometimes this feeling of guilt gives rise to a whole range of psychological problems. And instead of strengthening your focus on your child and family in order to correct your past mistakes, you plunge into depression and even start to feel fear of Divine punishment.

Beloved, God does not want to punish you. He wants you to realize your mistakes and not to repeat them in the future. There is no sinner without a future. And sometimes a person who has realized his mistakes and repented for them can do much more for humankind than a person who does not commit any improper acts because of fear of Divine punishment.

Direct your energy to a positive path! Do not chew over the scenes of your past sins and mistakes again and again. That will only make matters worse because you will be directing energy to the same wrong path. The river of the Divine energy that flows through you should find a new channel and wash away the consequences of all the past wrong states of consciousness.

Constantly concentrating on the positive and on a desire to help those around you, especially your children, can transform the energy of past mistakes and create a new opportunity for the future of your children.

Complete realization of past mistakes and a fervent desire not to repeat them are quite enough to change the karmic consequences and create a bright future for your children.

Do not forget that you have created karmic connections with your children. And there is a strong probability that in your future incarnations you will be the children of those individuals who are your children now. In order to alleviate your karma in the future, you should primarily be concerned about the souls of your children now.

Everything in the world is interconnected, and you need to be very careful and thoughtful about everything that you do.

The purpose of my talk today was to give you the knowledge about the importance of a thoughtful approach to planning a child's birth. In fact, you create your own future and the future of the whole planet at the moment of conception of your child. Think about that the next time you satisfy your sexual desire.

**I AM Kuthumi,
with care for your souls and the souls
of all living beings.**

Some comments on the Laws of Karma and Reincarnation

June 28, 2012

I AM Kuthumi.

Yet again, the subject of our discourse today will be your consciousness because there is nothing more important for you at this time. Your consciousness is something that brings you closer to God or moves you away from God. Thus, everything in your life is determined by the level of your consciousness.

Therefore, let us quietly consider eternal topics.

Before my arrival to you, I had a talk with the Messenger in my retreat. During this conversation I tried to understand how I can possibly better convey to you the tasks that are on the agenda for incarnated humanity. And you know, I was surprised to discover that all that knowledge and understanding that needed to be conveyed to you, we had already brought during the period of

Dictations that we had been giving you periodically and in a measured way through our Messenger for the last eight years.

I have nothing to add to what has been said.

Only to support today's conversation and use the Divine opportunity, I will repeat some truths for those who came to familiarize themselves with today's Message.

I come again and again, and our conversations remind me of how I am trying to find and show you the subtle processes that are taking place in your consciousness with the help of the finest tools: tweezers and a brush. Step by step, I show you how you need to behave in this or that situation in order to save a particle of God within you and to establish immediate, direct contact with it.

How surprised I am sometimes when, after our talks, you expose your being to a garbage dump of human imperfections, including television or participation in some kind of mass entertainment.

You can imagine what a huge pile of garbage of mass consciousness you let into your subconsciousness at any mass event, along with poor-quality music and low vibrations that penetrate inside of you along with the smell of roasted meat or alcohol.

Our talks with you and your leisure amusements with television and masses of people have different weight categories. And you must decide and clarify for yourself once and for all in which direction you intend to move: in the direction of the summit of the Divine consciousness or the garbage heap of history.

No, I cannot forbid and I cannot deprive you of any of your amusements or any of your sweet attachments. Only you yourself can make a decision and act according to it. My task is simply to give you the knowledge and understanding of what will happen to you in either case.

Notice that I am not scaring you or forcing you in any way. We are just having a nice talk, and I am explaining to you the consequences of your actions.

One of the main cornerstones of the Teaching being given is the Law of Karma and the Law of Reincarnation because everything else is a consequence of these two fundamentals of the Teaching.

For example, nobody will come out to forbid your free disposition of your sexual energy. You can afford any misuse. However, you must understand that the more uncontrollably you waste your sexual potential, the less vital energy you have to continue the evolution. Your descendants will be weaker, if it is possible for them to appear at all, and you will burden yourself and all your close relatives with more diseases.

Where does this lead? This leads to degradation and degeneration. And within only several generations from a healthy cell of society, your family and your kin will turn into hapless and sick people who are not capable of further evolution.

If you want your family to prosper, and if you want to have excellent health for the rest of your life, then you are destined for chastity and abstinence. As you can see, I am not inventing anything; I am just logically clarifying the operation of the Law of Karma or Retribution for you.

If we consider the Law of Reincarnation in more detail, then with a strong probability you will have an incarnation in the same family that you are incarnated now. And if you do not care about morality in your family, then in several decades you will have your incarnation in the same family, but this family will be burdened with a large number of diseases, many of which will be incompatible with the continuation of life. That is how extinction and degeneration occur to those who do not follow the Divine Law but follow the law of mass consciousness that is now acceptable in your society.

Believe me, not much time will pass by earthly standards, and all the followers of mass consciousness will be forced to drag out a miserable existence somewhere in reservations for inferior people, like the habitats for the savages of Australia.

If you do not wish to find yourselves at the roadside of evolution, then you will have to start following our recommendations that we are giving, including through these Messages of ours.

I have given you a very important talk today. And this talk is all the more opportune, the less time remaining for humankind as a whole to decide which path to follow: the one that the Ascended Masters teach humankind or the one that is strenuously imposed through mass media.

I am very much expecting that at least one-tenth of the people who will familiarize themselves with this Message of mine will seriously consider the effects on their consciousness of the many things that are freely promoted in society but are not as useful to your being as our Messages.

I AM Kuthumi.

Divine Truth is comprehended not by external research but by inner searching

June 28, 2013

I AM Kuthumi. Today we will consider a few statements of the Teaching that are given to humanity of Earth by the Masters of Wisdom.

It required a certain time for me to be able to come closer to you through the worlds. The process of interaction between the worlds, as well as the process of transmission of our Messages, is still not adequately explored by secular science. It is also due to the fact that science is biased against everything that deals with the supernatural from a scientific point of view and that is unexplainable in terms of the physical world and its laws. Some time will pass and the boundaries of cognition of the world through science will expand, and the subdivision that exists in contemporary science will take a broader view regarding the Subtle worlds. However, this will not happen any sooner than when the most progressive minds of humanity believe in our existence and establish regular contact with us.

A permanent contact with us is possible only if you are sincere and truly believe in our existence. And even this is not enough, because in addition to faith, you must be devoted to the Brotherhood and meet the conditions on the basis of which we have been working with humanity for a long period of time.

Those of you who are familiar with the abundant esoteric literature have most likely noticed the fact that this category of literature is of two significantly different types, or kinds.

The first kind of esoteric literature includes various types of psychic research of people who work mostly with the astral plane and with the lowest layers of the mental plane. These are the impressions of the undeveloped consciousness about the Subtle worlds, and frankly speaking, the morbid reflection of many things of the Subtle layers close to the physical world in the consciousness of particular individuals. This is a huge collection of literature that you can absolutely quite easily bypass without paying any attention to it. Moreover, I strongly recommend that you do not get involved in reading this kind of literature, because it can cause damage to your psyche as it submerges you in the morbid vibrations of someone's fantasies.

The other kind of esoteric literature is extremely rare in your world, and at present it is more of a random phenomenon than a regular standard. This is understandable since the proportion of 10 percent of truth to 90 percent of lies is currently valid for your world at present and is applicable to the case with esoteric literature as well.

Here I must make a slight amendment. Due to the fact that currently the opposing forces have intensified their resistance, the true esoteric literature may be found on your shelves even more rarely. The proportion of one percent to 99 percent is already optimistic.

And even when you find, from our point of view, pure sources of information, you must be cautious and try to carefully check the publication that you are holding in your hands with the help of your intuition. Many well-known authors and their works, having passed through the fraudulent hands of some editors, metamorphose to an extent beyond recognition, and the percentage of truth in this printed product decreases, and it becomes very difficult to determine where there are inclusions of vibrations and energies extraneous to us.

Therefore, from the viewpoint of the majority of people, it is very fair to abandon reading esoteric literature as a whole because at the current pace of modern living, people simply have no time to examine the bulk of surrogates that are abundantly introduced on the shelves of shops and on the Internet.

However, even here you are in danger. By refusing to understand what has not yet anchored in the collective consciousness of humanity and has not acquired authenticity for the majority of human society, you risk missing a chance to use the knowledge and recommendations that are genuinely true and are given by us, the Ascended Masters, and are indispensable for the current stage of the evolutionary development of humanity.

The reader must stop in perplexity at this point in our discourse because, most likely, one question has been itching in his mind for quite a long while, "What is he driving at?"

Indeed, the situation is deplorable. On the one hand, we are trying to extend a helping hand to humanity to render assistance in the escape from a seeming impasse in which humanity of Earth finds itself. On the other hand, due to the activation of opposing forces at the current moment of time, the informational field of the planet is so littered that it is almost impossible to distinguish between the truth and the lies.

There is a way out of any situation. So, there is a way out of this situation as well. The solution for this situation lies on the surface. Everything in your world is attracted according to vibrations. Therefore, with unerring accuracy you will find in the world around you exactly what corresponds to your vibrations. If your vibrations are low, no matter how hard you try to come closer to the true source of information, you will fail.

But the opposite statement is also true: If your vibrations are high, then no matter how hard you try to find a book or a source of information that is disharmonious with your vibrations, you will not succeed.

What am I calling you to do during our discourse today? I do hope that everyone who reads this Message of mine does it exactly because the level of their vibrations permits them to read this Message.

Now all you have to do is to take the following step: Stop.

Stop your spiritual search.

This does not mean that you should stop your real spiritual search. You must only stop looking through various sources of information in the outer world.

If your intuition tells you that you have found the true source, then stop trying the other sources. Stay with one source and drink the water only from it.

It is possible to draw an analogy with your physical world. Let us suppose you are searching for a spring in a valley to quench your thirst. You taste the water from the spring and you are surprised at its crystal purity and perfect taste.

Wise people will stop at this spring and drink, and they will also make a supply of this water in their reservoirs and vessels.

People with less wisdom will go and try tasting water from another source. The water in that source will be bitter and salty. Then they will go to the next spring. The water in that source will turn out to be stagnated. Then they will proceed to another spring, and the water there will be dirty. Eventually, these people run the risk of never coming back to the spring with pure water, and they will continue roaming and drinking dirty water.

Therefore, when you understand with your whole being that a pure source of Divine Truth is before you, never look for other sources. Because Divine Truth is one, it is not comprehended by external research but by inner searching.

It is necessary to pass from the external to the inner knowledge. The external is only an impulse for your consciousness to enable you to plunge into the space of communication with God, who resides within your own being.

I have probably wearied you with my discourse today. However, I do expect that those few for whom I have given this Message of mine will hear me and take advantage of my advice.

I AM Kuthumi.

If you do not think about God, then you separate yourselves from God

December 26, 2013

I AM Kuthumi.

I have come today in order to talk about the main thing that is vital for you at this period of time.

What do you think is most essential for you now?

Many people will say that the main thing for them is money. Others will say that it is health.

Some will say that they lack for a feeling of love that they could experience for another person.

There are many things you would like to possess in your life, and they seem most essential to you.

I will not argue with any of you, because you choose by yourselves what things to do in your lives. And I have not come to persuade you that the things you do in your lives are incorrect or wrong.

I have come to remind you of what is most essential for you, and this important thing is no longer in the lives of the majority of incarnated humankind. Of course, I am talking about your Oneness with God.

The feeling of your Oneness with God, with God within yourselves, within your family, your friends, and the sense of Oneness with God in every particle of Life — this feeling is lost by humanity.

If you could restore this unity, then each of you would be happy and peaceful. You would feel your perfect security and peace.

I have solved, then, the truth about what you are actually lacking in your lives, haven't I?

You may name it differently, but it is the unity with the Creator of this Universe and with His manifestation in each particle of Life that you are sorely lacking in your lives now.

Why did it happen?

Why did you lose your Oneness?

Why do you feel alone and unprotected?

Why is fear the prevailing feeling in your society?

I am ready to answer these questions in this Message of mine.

That is why I have come.

To begin with, you yourselves are the cause of the separation from the Divine world. You probably have heard many times that you are to blame for everything that happens to you. Of course, this is the basic statement of the fundamental Law of this Universe — the Law of Karma or retribution.

Everything that we have in the present is caused by our past choices and actions. It means that you yourselves were the cause of the state that you and society are now in, at this moment in time.

A long time ago, you took the first step directed away from the Oneness inherent in you. That step was directed toward separation. You chose to create your own destiny. And you chose to act according to your desires and inclinations.

According to the Law of free will, your actions were absolutely correct. You tried to manifest your individuality in accordance with its inherent inclinations and talents.

This moment of your choice took place millions of years ago. Since then the material world around you has been changing toward density. And now what you observe around you was, on a large scale, created by your consciousness and the actions that you have taken based on your free will.

Why do you not feel happy?

Why do you not feel joy?

Why are you not permeated with love, which is the feature of this Universe?

Doesn't this happen because you separated yourselves from the Divine world?

How many of you think about God during the day? About God who permeates the whole creation and who, in fact, you are in embodiment?

If you do not think about God, then you separate yourselves from God. And this separation of you yourselves from God is present in your consciousness.

We have come to a simple decision of how to return to you your Oneness with God and the associated states of tranquility, joy, happiness, and peace.

You only have to constantly think about God in order to bring Him back into your lives!

This decision is very simple: If you wish to be happy, be happy!

However, as soon as you make this simple decision in your consciousness and rush to implement it in your life, then literally miracles start to happen in your life: Everything around you begins to impede you from following your decision to become one with God. First, you are overwhelmed with your own thoughts. Your carnal mind starts giving you one idea after another.

Then you start thinking that it would be nice to go to the seaside for a rest before devoting your life to God. Or you think that it is too early for you to impose restrictions upon yourself because you suddenly start feeling love for your girlfriend or your boyfriend. Or you think that you have to earn a sufficient sum of money to have the opportunity to devote your life to God.

Your inner desires attract opportunities for you from space in order to manifest your desires. Your beloved calls you several months after your falling out. Or you are offered a profitable high-paying job. Or something else happens and you forget about God. You are immersed in your concerns and the experiences from the life around you.

Do not think that what I am telling you now is something bad or deserves public reprimand. No. This is a common situation that now has formed in the world. All of you who are in embodiment now are prisoners of the situation. You are trapped by the illusory forces.

If there were no way out of this labyrinth of the illusion, neither I nor any of the Masters would come to waste time giving our Messages.

However, I insist that each of you who read our Messages can, even in this incarnation, reduce the influence of the illusory forces to such an extent that those forces will no longer control and manipulate you, and you yourself will become the master of your destiny.

This is exactly why we come and provide instructions.

In fact, the liberation from the illusion is very simple. This liberation is completely in your consciousness.

You make a decision to free yourself from the influence of the illusory forces.

And you follow this decision of yours every day from morning until night.

If you always follow the same direction, you will reach your goal.

If you change the direction of your advancement every day — for example, in the morning you advance toward God and in the other half of the day you satisfy your desires, then you will never reach your goal: Oneness with God.

What impedes you most of all?

You yourselves.

You only have to overcome the resistance of your carnal mind. This is the main thing that you have to do. To do this, you have genuine spiritual practices that help you to keep your consciousness constantly directed toward God.

Every day you must devote some time for spiritual practices. You must not miss even a day, because if you stop pedaling while going up the mountain, you will slide down to the foot of the mountain and you will have to start your ascension again.

These are the main principles that will help you if you are determined to return to the state of your Oneness with God.

I AM Kuthumi.

The Path of a Mystic

At all times within the entirety of the religions of the world, there were people who stood independently from the official management of the church — venerable old men, yogis, prophets and mystics.

The official religion reckoned with the authority of some of them, but more often they were persecuted and even deprived of life.

Inside of each religion there are two approaches — an external path of following certain dogmas and rituals, and an inner path of search for an immediate personal communication with God.

Ninety percent of believers follow the first path. Very few people risk following the second path. It is a path of initiations, of secret knowledge, and of a personal mystical experience.

During the times described in history there existed secret schools of initiations on Earth. We know about the Pythagorean community, the Essene community, and the mystery school in Ancient Egypt.

At the end of 19th century, an attempt to give a part of secret knowledge to a wider audience was undertaken through H.P. Blavatsky and the Theosophical society.

In the 20th century the knowledge was given through Helena and Nicholas Roerich and later through a number of organizations in America: the Bridge to Freedom, the I AM Movement, and the Summit Lighthouse.

What is next?

In order to understand the meaning of at least the knowledge that was given through these people and these organizations, a constant presence of people who can keep their internal contact with God is necessary on Earth. It is extremely important right now when a lot of false teachers and psychics have appeared.

Someone must maintain the true, Divine vibration. Someone must constantly keep his consciousness in accordance with God. Only from this point of consonance with God is it possible to assess many events occurring on Earth now and to understand the knowledge that has already been given and written down on the pages of previous books.

I hope that many of the materials placed on the sites "Sirius" (www.sirius-ru.net and www.sirius-eng.net) will help to keep the inner guidelines and inner harmony with God inside of us.

Tatyana Mickushina

About the Messages and the Messenger

Since ancient times the Masters of Shambala were known in the East. In various teachings people call them by different names: the Teachers of Humanity, the Ascended Masters, the Masters of Wisdom, or the Great White Brotherhood.

These Teachers have reached the next stage of evolution and continue their development in the Higher planes. These Higher Beings consider it their duty to help humanity of Earth in the development of its consciousness.

The method that the Ascended Masters have chosen to communicate with humanity is the transmission of the Messages (Dictations) that are written by the Messenger, who has a special method that ensures the perception of the Messages from the higher, etheric octaves of Light.

H.P. Blavatsky, Helena and Nicholas Roerich, Mark and Elizabeth Prophet were such people.

In 2004, the Masters gave the mantle of their Messenger to Tatyana N. MICKUSHINA. The Messages transmitted through Tatyana N. Mickushina are published in a series of books called "Words of Wisdom." Twenty-one cycles of Messages containing more than 480 Dictations have been received over the last 12 years. The Messages have been translated into 20 languages. More than 60 books have been published during this period of time.

"I did all my best in order to perform my job of receiving the Messages. But in reality, everything was done by God.

"I never knew beforehand who of the Beings of Light would come to give a Message. I also did not know what the topic of the Message would be. And I still cannot understand how this miracle of the transmission of the Messages happens. The work of the receiving of the Messages is lying on the verge of human possibilities, and we can only guess how much effort the Ascended Hosts applied to make this many years' work successful." (T.N. Mickushina)

The information contained in the Messages does not belong to any particular system of beliefs or to any specific religion.

The Masters speak about the current historical moment on planet Earth. They tell us about energy and vibrations, about the illusion of this world and about the Divine Reality, about the Higher Self of a human and about his lower bodies. They familiarize us with the new facets of the Law of Karma (the Law of causes and effects) and the Law of Reincarnation. They give us concrete recommendations on how a person can change his own consciousness, so as not to be left on the roadside of the evolutionary path.

"...When you are equipped with the knowledge of the processes taking place, it will be easier for you to orientate yourselves and to endure the chaos that exists, but will soon be replaced by the new order.

"...The duration of the transitional period depends on how your inner confidence is in the fact that there are much more joyous and better times ahead for you.

"You have to change your consciousness and change your approach to everything that is around you. For the new age will be based on entirely new principles! And if you stick to fear, to individualism, to limitations, then you will be left behind; you will fail to keep up with the train of evolution.

"For team spirit, freedom and those relationships that are based on friendship and love will be characteristic of the new age!

"Transformation of consciousness and thinking — that is what must be done first of all! And the sooner you can transform your consciousness, the fewer calamities and difficulties mankind will face in the near future." (Saint Germain)

"We come time after time not to reveal a new Truth, but to enable you to remember the Ancient Truth that you knew long ago but forgot, since you have plunged into materiality too much. And now the time has come *to remember your Source and to return to it... This is the Truth that you learned in ancient Lemuria and Atlantis, in all the Mystery Schools of the past and the present that ever existed on Earth." (Serapis Bey)*

SANAT KUMARA · SHIVA · MORYA · MAITREYA · KUTHUMI

SAINT GERMAIN · MOTHER MARY · JESUS · GAUTAMA BUDDHA · PALLAS ATHENA

BOOKS BY
TATYANA N. MICKUSHINA
MASTERS OF WISDOM SERIES

Each of the Masters of Wisdom strives to give us what they consider most vital at the present moment of transition. Every message contains the energies of different Masters who give those messages. The Masters speak about the current historical moment on planet Earth. They tell us about energy and vibrations, about the illusion of this world and about the Divine Reality, about the Higher Self of a human and about his lower bodies. They give us concrete recommendations on exactly how to change our own consciousness and continue on the evolutionary Path. It is recommended that you prepare yourself for reading every message very carefully. You have to tune to the Master who is giving the message with the help of proper music, with the help of the Master's image, or by using a prayer or a meditation before reading the message. That way you align your energies, elevate your consciousness, and the messages can benefit you.

SANAT KUMARA

Masters of Wisdom, first of all Sanat Kumara, remind us about our Divine origin and call us to wake up to a Higher reality, because Divine Reality by its love, wisdom, and beauty exceeds any of the most wonderful aspects of our physical world. The Messages of Sanat Kumara include Teachings on true and false messengers, Communities of the Holy Spirit, responsibility for the duties that one has taken upon him/herself before their incarnation, the right use of the money energy, the choice of everyone between the Eternal and the perishable world, overcoming the ego, the Path of Initiations, and many other topics

MORYA

This book contains selected Messages from Master Morya. Many Teachings are given in the Messages, including the Teachings about the correct actions on the physical plane, Service to Brotherhood, the attainment of the qualities of a disciple such as devotion, persistence, aspiration, and discipline. Some aspects of the Teaching about changing of consciousness are also introduced here.

SHIVA

The present volume contains selected Messages of Lord Shiva. Many Teachings are given in these Messages; including the Teaching about God, the Teaching about Discernment of reality from illusion: which helps to ascend to a new level of consciousness and also new aspects of the Guru-chela relationship are considered.

SAINT GERMAIN

Saint Germain is at present an Ascended Master, the Hierarch of the New Age. In his last incarnation as the Count de Saint Germain in the 18th century, he exerted a great influence on the course of world history. The Messages of Master Saint Germain are charged with optimism and faith in the forthcoming Golden Age! He teaches about preparing for a New Age by transforming our consciousness, and reminds us: "Joy and Love come to you when your Faith is steadfast, when you rely in your consciousness on God and the Ascended Hosts."

MOTHER MARY

This book continues the Masters of Wisdom series of books. This series of books presents collections of Messages from different Masters who are most well-known to modern humanity. These Messages were transmitted through the Messenger Tatyana N. Mickushina, who has been working under the guidance of the Masters of Wisdom since 2004. Using a special method, T. N. Mickushina has received Messages from over 50 Beings of Light. Mother Mary is the Patroness of Russia. The Messages call for a review of the system of values and relationships in all spheres of life, to keep the consciousness in attunement with the Divine Reality; ways of raising the consciousness are given

JESUS

The book contains the Messages of Beloved Jesus. They give an in-depth the Teaching of Love for all Life, including to its enemies, the Teaching of Healing, the Teaching of the Inner Path, which lies in our hearts. Beloved Jesus gives knowledge of the Laws of Karma and Reincarnation, lost in modern Christianity, about the Kingdom of Heaven as a state of our consciousness.

GAUTAMA BUDDHA

The book contains the selected Messages of Gautama Buddha. Many Teachings are given in them.Here are some of the Teachings about: the change of consciousness, the current situation on the Earth, the interrelationship between cataclysms, social conflicts, wars and the level of consciousness of humanity, the Community, happiness, overcoming conflicts, discernment and Buddha consciousness.You can familiarize yourself with these and other Teachings in the Messages of the Great Teacher, given at the present stage to help people to overcome the critical situation on our planet.

PALLAS ATHENA

The book contains the messages of Pallas Athena. Here are some of the Teachings contained in the Messages of Pallas Athena: The manifestation of the Law of Karma; the elemental life; the onset of a new stage in the development of mankind; the overcoming of violence in the mind.

MAITREYA

Coming soon.

Author page of T. N. Mickushina on Amazon:
amazon.com/author/tatyana_mickushina

Masters of Wisdom

KUTHUMI

Dictations received by the Messenger
Tatyana Nicholaevna Mickushina
from 2005 through 2013

Tatyana N. Mickushina

Please, leave your review about this book at amazon.com. This will greatly help in spreading the Teaching of the Ascended Masters given through the Messenger Tatyana Mickushina.

Websites:

http://sirius-eng.net (English version)
http://sirius-ru.net (Russian version)

Books by T.N.Mickushina on amazon.com:
amazon.com/author/tatyana_mickushina

CPSIA information can be obtained
at www.ICGtesting.com
Printed in the USA
FSHW020944131019
62971FS